Think Again

Think Again: Transformation That Yields a Return on God's Investment

The Urban Ministry Institute
3701 East 13th Street North
Wichita, KS 67208

ISBN: 978-1-62932-508-8

Published by TUMI Press
A division of World Impact, Inc.

The Urban Ministry Institute is a ministry of World Impact, Inc.

THE URBAN MINISTRY INSTITUTE, *a ministry of* WORLD IMPACT, INC.

THINK AGAIN

Transformation That Yields a Return on God's Investment

DON ALLSMAN

TUMI Press • 3701 East 13th Street North • Wichita, Kansas 67208

To my wonderful children Ryan, Mark, and Janée,
I pray you will continue to make it your life's ambition to
participate in the Spirit's work to forge your identity in Christ,
producing a return on God's investment in your lives.

Don Allsman, 2018

THINK AGAIN

Table of Contents

Part III: You Participate

Appendices

THINK AGAIN

Introduction

Jesus wants to change the world through us!

But there is a problem. We get distracted from his purpose because we are preoccupied with ourselves.

Finding Identity

For contemporary Americans, "finding my identity" is in style. Some would go far to say that there is nothing more important in life than finding personal identity. The assumption is, "If I can figure out my identity, I can live in accordance with it, have a happy life, and be a whole person." Anyone who puts an obstacle in the way of that discovery will be criticized as grossly unfair.

People attempt to define themselves based on their ethnicity, sex, religion, class, generation, or a special interest. Those who are unsure of their identity have an "identity crisis." Identity politics is a recent term that is now embedded in the culture. But the pursuit of personal identity has not always been as prevalent as it is today. In fact, the notion of "finding identity" is relatively new.

For most cultures and generations, identity has been defined by the family, clan, or tribe to which they belonged, often associated with their family's role in the community (butcher, baker, or candlestick maker). None of these were matters of choice; a person was born into their identity. It then became each person's duty to pursue a virtuous life, serving the community by making sacrifices for the greater good. For centuries, what set an individual apart from others was some act of sacrificial heroism, not personal identity.[1]

This notion continued into 1940s America. But after World War II, everything changed. The proliferation of products and services led companies to emphasize self-expression over practicality. Buying a car was no longer about meeting a practical transportation need, but an expression of one's individual identity.[2] This opened the minds of Americans to a new way of thinking: purchasing products as a way to define their individual identity.

By the 1960s Americans rapidly lost interest in the traditional roles of duty, conformity, and community, turning instead to the pursuit of individuality and fame. Heroic sacrifice was replaced with the desire to become a *celebrity*, primarily by finding one's identity. And now, anyone who doesn't aggressively pursue their identity is seen as lacking character, and will be derisively called a zombie, drone, lemming, or sheep.

The Challenges of Finding Identity

For those who come from years of oppression, identity can be strongly associated with their struggle to be recognized as fully human. Prisoners, drug users, the abused, immigrants, or minorities live every day with the effects of their pain, and can start to believe they are nothing more than victims of their oppression. This adds another level of complexity in making sense of their identity.

While some will label themselves using a single identity ("I am Latino" or "I am a woman"), most people prefer to describe themselves as a unique composite of several personal interests. For example, "I am a Chevy-driving, Dodger-supporting, photography-loving, millennial, fitting the ENFJ Myers-Briggs profile, who likes drinking Mountain Dew." For others, identity is based on their role as a parent, or a passion they have like gardening or environmentalism. Sadly, some even frame their identity by living vicariously through sports teams or celebrities.

But it is difficult to "find myself" when there are so few absolutes in life. There are so many choices and not enough objective bases to make decisions. The more people pursue information, the more confused they become. So it becomes overwhelmingly complex to find personal identity. And once someone has successfully defined their identity, there is no rest, because they must work equally hard to *maintain* that identity.[3]

Narcissism

Since 1958, there has been an explosion of the number of people suffering from a vague, ill-defined anxiety, a dread that something is missing. More and more people have become self-absorbed with their infantile needs, producing a desire for instant gratification, which is called "narcissism."[4]

As affluent countries have become richer, received more leisure time, and enjoyed a higher standard of living, unhappiness has risen 20% and depression rates have increased 10-fold. In America, 15% now suffer from an anxiety disorder.[5] This is because Americans believe a lie: find your identity, you will be happy. After 50 years of chasing after personal identity, the result has been increased emptiness, worry, boredom, and addiction.

A Liar

The danger in finding personal identity is that we forget that there is an enemy who lies to us about who we are, an adversary who attempts to ruin our lives and take us off track. He would like to frame the debate of our identity and get us away from *our identity as God sees us*. He doesn't care what identity we choose, as long as it is not based in our identity in Christ.

So if your identity is based solely on being a social-justice advocate, Satan wins; a gang-banging drug lord, Satan wins; a greedy wall street mogul, Satan wins; a devoted grandmother, Satan wins. Identities don't have to be overtly evil to be satanic, they simply need to distract you from your true identity in Christ. Neil Anderson said, "We have been deceived into believing that what we do determines who we are. The only identity that works in God's Kingdom is you plus Christ equals wholeness and meaning."[6] If you do not know who you are in Christ, you will be defeated most of your life.[7]

Forging, not Finding

For the follower of Christ, there is a different path to identity. In the world, people attempt to *find their identity*, but in the Kingdom, God's desire is to *forge your identity* (Gal. 3.28). He wants to conform you to the image of Jesus (Rom. 8.29). Identity is not so much about discovering yourself, but realizing *who you belong to*.

You belong to a King with a kingdom task that is larger than yourself. It's not what you do that makes you meaningful, but the contribution you make for his Kingdom. You can be worthwhile when you can give up being a "big fish in little pond," accepting your role as a "little fish in God's grand ocean."

Jesus said you will find your life only when you lose it, when you give it up for his sake (Matt. 16.25). But when you permit

God to forge you, it doesn't mean you lose your personality or distinctiveness. Your are not *cloned*. God will reshape and transform you to live a Christian life that honors God and is true to yourself. You discover your calling and vocation, finding where you are on the map of life. Like the super heroes of comic book fame, in Christ you find your "true identity." As one of our leadership students from prison said, "In Christ, I met myself for the first time. I was existing, but now I'm living."

When God forges your identity, you realize you are much more than you appear to be.

Free at Last!

This realization provides confidence and joy! "Finding yourself" is not your responsibility. By allowing God to forge your identity in Christ, you can enjoy everything he provides for you (Chevys, Dodgers, photography, Myers-Briggs, Mountain Dew), without it *defining you*. When you no longer have to find yourself, you will be released from slavery to freedom. You can stand on another soil, breath another air, and look up to another sky. Your life motives can change, making your inward drives brand new.[8]

But securing this freedom is not easy, and it doesn't come in one fell swoop. Forging you into the character of Christ is a long and arduous process, superintended by the Spirit. For many, the process of deep, inward change is not desirable. We want instant change, and when we can't find it, we prefer to escape the problems of life through wealth, relationships, prestige, drugs, pornography, or shopping.

You can *find your identity*, or you can allow God to *forge your identity*. Finding or forging, that is the question. If you are ready to say "yes" to the Spirit's forging work, the next chapters will be helpful.

The Forging Process

Part I: The Enemy Pillages describes the devil's strategies to oppose God's work. This section reveals his schemes to steal, kill, and destroy that result in strongholds and distortion of our true identity.

Part II: God Provides celebrates the warm and generous nature of the Triune God who gives us abundant life through the Father's philanthropy, the Son's potential, and the Spirit's power. This section also explores the metaphor of God as *venture capitalist*, seeking a return on his investment (ROI) in us.

Part III: You Participate provides a road map for you to participate in God's work to forge your identity into the image of Christ. Although the enemy pillages and God provides, *you* participate in the forging of your identity, all for the end goal of returning an investment for God.

Here is the crux of the matter: You can try to find inner calm, power, and poise by controlling the circumstances of life, or you can let God shape you on the inside so that no matter what happens, nothing can sink you.[9] Can you imagine a future where God is at work within you in such a way that no matter what happens in life you can be secure? You can become *unsinkable*!

A Sequel of Sorts

In my book *Jesus Cropped from the Picture*, I was critical of an over-emphasis on a "personal relationship with Christ." However in this book, my sole attempt is to help you live out a personal relationship with Jesus. In that way, *Think Again* is a sequel to *Jesus Cropped from the Picture*. People have told me that *Jesus Cropped from the Picture* was helpful, but wished I had said more about what they could do personally. *Think Again* is my attempt to meet their request.

I pray that you will allow God to do his work of producing abundant fruit in your life. Just think what refreshment awaits the people in your world if you can be forged to the very identity of the Lord Jesus Christ! This book is not just for you, but for untold people waiting to be blessed by you.

THINK AGAIN

Part I: The Enemy Pillages

The thief comes to steal, kill, and destroy.

John 10.10a

THINK AGAIN

CHAPTER 1

The US Government Will Do That

Anyone who has played high school basketball is familiar with running lines, a conditioning drill where one runs from the baseline to the free-throw line and back; to half-court and back; to the far free-throw line and back, and finally to the other end line and back. It seemed that my coaches delighted to see us suffer, yelling at us to "run faster," until we were ready to keel over. Some of us would go as hard as we could, while others gave only a half-hearted effort. When my coach observed even one person slacking off, he would punish all of us by making us run more. It was a dreadful experience.

During these years I started suffering from a recurring nightmare. Awakened from a peaceful sleep, I dreamt my coach was in my room shouting, "Allsman, what are you doing sleeping when you should be out there running!!" I would jump out of bed, stand at my bedside (for who knows how long), and then eventually realize that it was not real. Then I would go back to sleep only to wake up again haunted by the same dream.

Years later, these stress dreams took a comical turn when I married my wife, Cathy.

We hadn't been married long when Cathy felt something bumping her side. She woke and saw me raising and lowering my arms in unison, and said, "What are you doing?!" Without waking up, I responded, in between deep breaths, "Pumping . . . iron." I immediately realized I had been doing bench presses in my sleep. I had no idea how long this had been going on. It was only when Cathy spoke that I became aware of the fictional world in which I was living.

A few months later, we moved to Wichita, Kansas where we both went to graduate school. It was a cold winter night, and being college students who were unable to afford to heat the apartment at night, we relied on many layers of blankets to keep us warm. Feeling a cold draft, Cathy woke up to see me slowly pulling the covers off the bed. She said, "What are you doing?!" I abruptly whispered, "Shhhhhh. There's a snake in the bed." She said, "You are dreaming again, give me the blankets back and go to sleep." Cathy made several earnest attempts to assure me of our safety before I allowed her to have the covers back. It seemed so real!

Some years later, we moved back to California. Cathy had one of those feelings people have when they sense someone is in the room. She switched on her bedside light to find me standing in the corner of the bedroom in my swim trunks, with my hands on my hips. She asked her oft-repeated question, "What are you doing?!" As she spoke, I woke up, looked around for a moment and replied, "I have no idea."

The funny part of this story is the amount of effort this must have taken on my part. My swim trunks were hidden away for the winter, so that means I got up in my sleep, rifled through my clothes until finding them, changed into them from my warm pajamas, and stood in the corner of the chilly bedroom. I may have stood there all night had Cathy not rescued me from my misadventure.

One early morning I had a dream that Cathy wanted a cold washcloth for her forehead. So I walked to the sink, soaked a washcloth with cold water, and returned to present it to my dear wife. In my dream, she hadn't asked me to wring it out first, so as I quietly said, "Here's the washcloth you wanted," ice-cold drops of water fell on her face. She quickly whacked it out of my hand, sending it flying across the room exclaiming, "What are you doing?!" Feeling wounded by her ungrateful attitude, I said, "I brought you the cold washcloth you asked for." Wiping water from her face, she said, "You're dreaming again. Get that thing away from me and go back to bed."

My favorite stress-dream story comes in the historical context of the confirmation hearings for Supreme Court Justice Clarence Thomas. It was a big news story at the time, and captured much of my attention. One night, I bolted up in bed and said, "Oh no!!!!" Concerned there was an intruder or some kind of emergency, Cathy exclaimed, "What's wrong?" I said, "If they confirm Clarence Thomas, I'll have to put him on the payroll!" After enduring several years of my annoying dreams, Cathy had learned how to handle the situation. She calmly said, "You don't need to do that Don, the US government will handle that for you." Relieved by her words, I said, "Oh good" and went back to sleep.

Feelings Unconnected to Reality

Not everyone has amusing and embarrassing stories like mine, but there is a fundamental element that we all share as humans. *All of us are subjected to thoughts and feelings that have no connection to reality.* Our enemy the devil constantly bombards us with confusing messages that are disconnected from God's truth. He lies, deceives, and distorts so that we might live in confusion and distraction.

Like my stress dreams, the enemy's lies can seem real and based on sound experience. I really thought there was a snake in the bed. I really thought it was my job to put Clarence Thomas on the payroll. I really thought Cathy wanted a cold, dripping washcloth. And the troubling part is that my body reacted to my dreams as though the delusions were true. My adrenaline was pumping at the same rate as if a snake were really in the bed. My anxiety about Clarence Thomas produced the same destructive effect on my body as though I really were failing at my job. And when Cathy told me the federal government would care for Clarence Thomas, my body reacted as though it was true. I calmed down and went back to sleep.

Your body cannot tell the difference between truth and lies. If you believe there is a snake in the bed, your body will react as though it were true and react with a burst of adrenaline. If you don't believe there is a snake in the bed, your body will relax and you can sleep peacefully. There is no such thing as "truth" and "lies" when it comes to your body's nervous system.

The reality is that you react to whatever you *believe*. If you tell yourself something enough times, you will start to believe it, whether it is true or not. "I am dumb and I can't do anything right" can start off as a joke but after repeating it enough, you begin to believe it. If you tell yourself you have no interests, soon you will find yourself having no interests.[10] Over time, who you *think* you are, actually becomes *who* you are.

So your spiritual and physical health is dependent upon what you *believe*. If you believe Satan's accusations, your body will respond to those accusations as though they were true. When the adversary suggests, "God has abandoned you and you are alone," if you *believe* that lie, your body will suffer anxiety leading to bitterness, worthlessness, disappointment, and fear. On the other hand, when Satan says, "God has abandoned you," you can *believe* what God says in his Word, affirming that you are cherished and forgiven. If you believe God's truth, your body will respond in joy and thanksgiving.

Expose Lies and Affirm Truth

Because your body reacts to your *belief*, your job is to expose lies and affirm truth. Lies and truth have no power in themselves; they are neutral. You activate lies or truth by what you *believe*. You can expose the lies of the deceiver and affirm the truth of God's Word.

Because your body reacts so strongly to what you believe, the accuser can trick you into believing the same lies over and over until they form toxic habits and attitudes. At first he brings lies that set off frantic alarms inside, but after repeated practice, you will no longer be able to turn the alarms off. You will start living in a constant state of panic. When you agree with the devil's deceptions, you etch grooves in your brain that, in time, form strongholds. By so doing, you slowly destroy your own life and negatively impact the people around you.

On the other hand, if you believe what God's Word says, the Spirit will change your habits and attitudes to be like the Lord Jesus. This enables you to glorify God and bless others for his sake. He can forge your identity, being conformed to his likeness (Rom. 8.29). As Neil Anderson said, "As believers, we are not trying to become saints; we are saints who are becoming like Christ."[11] When you agree with the truth of God's Word, you demolish old strongholds and forge new habits that bring life and peace.

You can change from the inside out, transforming to become more like Jesus. This means you don't simply have to "try harder to avoid sin," but by the work of the Spirit, you can be transformed into a different person on the inside. By forging identity, you can change what you believe and how you react!

Part A

Jesus said about the adversary, "The thief comes only to steal and kill and destroy" (John 10.10a). He is a pillager, a robber, and a murderer. He attempts to thwart God's work and ruin our lives at the same time. Sometimes we miss the violent nature of the devil's agenda. He did not come to "tickle, bump, and annoy" but to "steal, kill and destroy." He is a vicious and powerful adversary prowling around for someone to devour (1 Pet. 5.8). His desire is chaos and devastation.

He employs the arithmetic of *subtraction*, taking valuables away from people. He is the kind of bully who steals lunch money from a child or steps on a flower. He constantly pillages, manifested in rejection, sickness, interpersonal conflicts, financial problems, and wars. The Bible frequently refers to these as coming from "the world, the flesh, and the devil" (e.g. Eph. 2.1-3, James 4.1-7), but we recognize all evil originating from a single source: Satan. Paul said the evil one is an enemy of all righteousness, full of deceit and villainy, perverting the ways of the Lord (Acts. 13.10).

Part B

In spite of the accuser's devastating efforts to steal, kill, and destroy, God offers an entirely different approach. There is a "Part B" to John 10.10. Jesus contrasts the enemy's pillaging work by declaring that we can have *abundant life*. While the devil's math is based on *subtraction*, God's math is rooted in *multiplication*. Where the evil one tries to steal your lunch money, God wants to give you enough money for your own lunch, plus a little extra something so you can treat your friends to lunch too (Eph. 4.25).

God wants to forge your identity so he can multiply the blessings of his Kingdom. He wants a return on his investment (ROI). If you consider the themes of Jesus's parables you will see that this is true.

- Parable of the Talents (Matt. 25.14-30): God gives talents and expects to receive more than he put in.
- Parable of the Soils (Matt. 13.3-9): God provides the seed and expects 30, 60, 100 times the investment.
- Parable of the Mustard Seed (Matt. 13.31-32): A small seed results in a large plant that provides refuge for others.
- Parable of Leaven (Matt. 13.33): A small amount of leaven spreads to whole loaf.

In all these parables, God provides the seed and expects a harvest well beyond what he put in. He makes the initial investment, but asks you to produce a windfall. Because Jesus appointed you to bear fruit that will last (John 15.16), there is work for you to do. As he forges your identity, he wants you enhance your ability to yield an ROI for him.

The reason Jesus came was to destroy the works of the devil (1 John 3.8). Now you become Jesus's agent to carry on the destruction of Satan's works. The enemy pillages and God provides, but you participate in God's work to frustrate the enemy, advancing God's Kingdom.

THINK AGAIN

CHAPTER 2

I Don't Think I Want to Be a Part of This Confrontation

Our son Mark has always been a source of funny stories. From a young age, he has said surprising things that caught us off guard, using vocabulary that seemed beyond the understanding of someone his age.

When he was six years old, I announced the convening of a family meeting. Right away, his older brother Ryan (age 11 at the time) inferred by the tone of my voice that this was going to be an unpleasant meeting. Oblivious to the non-verbal cues, Mark excitedly said, "Are we going to go to a movie or going out for dinner?"

Before I could respond, Ryan whispered to Mark that this event was going to be serious. Mark's countenance dropped and said, "I don't think I want to be a part of this confrontation."

Cathy and I burst out laughing, wondering if Mark even knew what a "confrontation" was.

The Epic Battle

When it comes to the epic battle we find ourselves in, we can feel the same way Mark did. Sometimes we wish we hadn't landed in the middle of a confrontation between God and the devil. We wish we could avoid it, or negotiate a truce with the enemy.

But it is comforting to realize that there is an historical context to our situation. Our day-to-day existence is part of something far bigger than just our personal problems. Dallas Willard said, "Instead of being the main show, we are of significance only as a – very important – part of an immense struggle between immense forces of good and evil."[12] This gives us the right perspective to cope with the realities of life.

This is a battle that preceded us, and goes on after we die. Before Creation, the devil rebelled against God and then recruited Adam and Eve into rebellion at the Fall. Ever since that day, God has been intent to win back everything that was lost at the Fall. Through Jesus our Lord, the devil was defeated in his incarnation, his miracles, his exorcisms, his death and resurrection, and his ascension. He sent the Holy Spirit at Pentecost to launch the Church and begin the process of expanding his kingdom influence around the world.

The "gospel" is the good news that God will prevail in this broader historical conflict. Before you understood the gospel, your eyes were blind to much of what was happening in the invisible world all around you. But when God revealed himself, the Spirit entered and gave you the ability to understand his Word, including:

- A Creator and his creation
- A plan designed by God the Father
- A Champion working to make all things new, the Lord Jesus
- An invitation to receive forgiveness and join him in his work

- An adversary who attempts to keep everyone from understanding the truth

The battlefield location of this war between God and Satan is *your mind.* Your mind is the nexus of cosmic struggle. The human mind is the bull's-eye of Satan's target. He looks at you through the cross-hairs of his weapons scope, because if he can rule your mind, he can keep you from being effective for Christ.

He Lost His Grip Forever

Once you were blinded to this "real world." But now that God has opened your eyes, the adversary has lost you forever to the Kingdom of Light. Because of that defeat, he turns all his energy to tricking you into squandering the treasures God gives you. He pivots from keeping you *blinded* to keeping you *distracted.* He wants to mess with your mind so you don't live as a true child of God. He puts down his weapons of blinding and picks up new weapons of distraction, disruption, discouragement, and dismay.

The accuser uses us like pawns to frustrate God's work. He pillages with ruthlessness and cunning. In *A Mighty Fortress Is Our God*, Luther said, "For still our ancient foe doth seek to work us woe, his craft and power are great, and armed with cruel hate, on earth is not his equal." Satan wants to destroy us and grieve God in the process. But we are only tools in his larger game. He cares nothing about us.

He tries to take what rightfully belongs to us, but if he can incite us to destroy ourselves, all the better for him. So he is a master of deception. Jesus called him "the father of lies" (John 8.44). No one is exempt from his methods, and no one can live a single day without being in the middle of this spiritual confrontation.

But God has a different agenda. C. S. Lewis talked about Jesus as a King who landed in disguise and has invited us to join in a great work of sabotage.[13] As the people of his story, God uses us to carry on his work of sabotage. Luther said, "And though this world, with devils filled, should threaten to undo us, we will not fear, for God hath willed his truth to triumph through us."

On one side, the adversary erects strongholds to keep us bound, rendering us ineffective in God's sabotage. On the other side, God is constantly providing truth, encouragement, and comfort to make us increasingly fruitful, eager to produce a return on his investment.

For his part, the deceiver employs a three-step strategy to distract us: devaluing, globalizing, and irrationality.

Devaluing

The accuser starts by speaking false statements and doubts into our minds. They are vicious and devastating, striking at our deepest fears. Jennings said, "Every human being descended from Adam and Eve is born infected with fear and selfishness – fear of failure, fear of what others think, fear of not getting that job, fear of not getting that guy or girl, fear of not getting that grade, fear of not being loved, fear of being alone, fear, fear, fear!"[14]

The enemy analyzes you, sizes you up, and designs a line of attack that plays on your fears. Here are a few examples:

- You don't belong.
- No one loves you. You are lonely and miserable.
- You have no talent or gifting. There's no hope for you.
- Look at her, why can't you be like her?
- God doesn't really love you or this bad thing wouldn't have happened.

- You're not really a Christian – look at what you just did.
- No one is going to talk to you at the party because you are a loser.
- They don't respect you because you don't deserve respect.
- Even when you try your best to find a boyfriend/girlfriend, no one is interested in you.
- You'll never change.

Boom, boom, boom; every day you are bombarded by the incessant, constant pounding of lies to devalue yourself. In fact, he disguises his message by making them seem like they are *your own ideas*, not his.[15] Designing a personalized attack strategy, he chips away you. He knows what is effective on you won't work on me, and what works on me won't be tempting to someone else. Every single human has enough fears for the evil one to formulate an effective, individualized devaluation strategy. But devaluing is just the first stage.

Globalizing

Once you agree with his lies, he has gained a foothold and will proceed to globalize your situation:

- Since you failed this time, you will *always* fail.
- Since you feel lonely now, you will *always* feel lonely.
- Since you are divorced, no one will *ever* love you again.
- Since your spouse yelled at you, you'll *never* have a good marriage.
- Nothing goes right with you, *everything* you touch fails.
- Because no one talked to you at the party, *no one will ever* talk to you at a party again.

Irrationality

If you believe his globalizing efforts, he can move to the next phase: suggest you accept irrational conclusions:

- I need to be perfect *all the time*, or I'll never get respect.
- *Everyone* is against me.
- If I don't meet *everyone's* expectations, I'll never have friends.
- If I don't make this ministry happen, my life will be *ruined*.
- Since I don't have a boyfriend/girlfriend, my life is *over*.
- I'll never make it in life; it's *hopeless*.
- Life has to be fair and just *all the time*.
- If my kids don't turn out, it will show that *I was a bad parent*.
- If my family suffers it will be *my fault*.
- *Why even try?*

Devaluing, globalizing, and irrationality: This is the pattern that erects strongholds. With shame, I offer a personal example.

One day a trusted colleague named Paul wrote me an email about the possibility of changing offices. Satan started twisting this by saying, "Paul doesn't respect you or he wouldn't ask you to change offices." I believed it (devaluing). Then the accuser said, "Other people don't respect you either." I believed that one too (globalizing). Then finally, "Everyone always disrespects you, all the time. You should resign from the ministry." I believed that one as well (irrationality).

I agitated about this all night long, missing out on a good night's sleep. When I finally talked to Paul about it, he said he had no intention of showing disrespect and was more or less just "thinking out loud." To my embarrassment, I let the enemy work me over through devaluing, globalizing, and irrationality.

Constant Rampage

Every day, all day long, every single human being on earth is presented with thousands of thoughts and feelings that rampage through their minds if left unchecked. The deceiver never takes a day off. He never leaves anyone alone. If he would tempt the Lord Jesus with lies, you can be sure he won't leave you alone either. You can be the most secure and Godly person and he will still throw false messages at you every day.

The effect of believing these lies takes on many forms: anxiety, depression, mental illness, physical maladies, and broken relationships. The enemy's pillaging extends even to suicide, which occurs every 12 seconds. For every person who succeeds, 25 others attempt to take their own life.[16] That means that the accuser convinces two people to kill themselves every second. He steals, kills, and destroys in dramatic ways.

Although most people don't go so far as considering suicide, nearly everyone is consumed by keeping up appearances, terrified of what others think. The enemy whispers words of fear, "You are a fraud and people are going to find out." So we waste time and energy trying convince people to think well of us. We fear looking foolish, being useless, or becoming destitute. And because of those fears, we are constantly vulnerable to lies.

Strongholds Are Built

All we really want in life is to be loved, accepted, and to do meaningful work. We just want to count for something. God is ready to fulfill these godly desires, but the enemy provides a twisted alternative, a false solution that leaves God out of the equation and puts the sole responsibility on us.

Like Adam and Eve, we think, "Maybe God can't be trusted for my physical needs," so like our ancestors we see that the fruit is *good for food* and we reach for it.

"Maybe God can't be trusted to give me a happy life," so we see that the fruit is a *delight to the eyes* and we reach for it.

"I wonder if God is keeping me in the dark, making me look foolish," so we see that the fruit would *make us wise* and we reach for it.

We pick the fruit of these temptations and eat them, dozens of times each day. As we do, we cause damage to ourselves and others, doing nothing to reduce our insecurities. In fact, our fears often get worse.

When lies are offered to us, and we consume them without cross-examination, they form an attitude. Over time these attitudes become a normal part of our thinking. Therefore, by our acceptance of those lies, a stronghold is built *one bite at a time*.

Signs of Strongholds

Here are a few signs that you have allowed a stronghold to take place:

- You become hard on the outside but fearful on the inside. As Dr. Don Davis says, "You act like The Incredible Hulk, but inside you feel like Winnie the Pooh."
- You chronically speak negatively about yourself. "Nothing ever goes right for me. Everything I touch fails."
- You worry about things that haven't happened yet and may never happen.
- Anxiety or bitterness floods your daily thoughts and then they come out of your mouth (Matt. 15.18).

- You are busy trying to earn God's favor. You live in regret, defeat, and condemnation rather than the loving encouragement that God provides. "For godly grief produces a repentance that leads to salvation *without regret*" (2 Cor. 7.10).
- You speak often about "if-only." If only I could get a job I like, then life would be good. If I just had more friends, I could be content. If I just had better parents, I would be more well-adjusted. If I just could get over this illness, I'd be happy. If I only had a better degree, I'd be respected.

If you believe his devaluing lies, then globalize them, and allow them to develop to an irrational level, you construct a stronghold that is difficult to demolish (see examples, Appendix 1). After the constant barrage of the enemy, you can feel like a huge pile of scrap metal: scattered, broken, useless.

No one can escape the accuser's intrusion into your thoughts. But not every thought that pops in your head is true. You don't have to be victimized by entertaining the ideas that invade your mind. God has a better way. He provides insight about the schemes of the devil (2 Cor. 2.11), so you can recognize deception and *Think Again* about truth.

THINK AGAIN

CHAPTER 3

Con Artists and Rodents

Evil spirits are constantly at work to dispossess us. They want us to relinquish our treasures by our own free will. Their activities can be understood using two familiar pillaging metaphors: rodents and con artists.

Rodents

Demons are like rats, in that they need garbage to feed on.[17] When you leave garbage unattended in your life, you give evil spirits an entry point, an invitation to make infestation worse. When you let worry, lust, greed, and bitterness pile up inside, you give the devil opportunity to invade your life (Eph. 4.27). By letting them remain, they become like a growing pile of trash that invites even more attacks from the enemy.

To get rid of rats, the trash has to be taken away. This requires a process of forging identity over time; it is not a one-shot deal. Removing the garbage is achieved through the transforming work of the Spirit. As each bit of refuse is removed, you gain strength and discourage future infestations.

The adversary knows that whatever you meditate on will grow, for good or bad. If you interpret events in light of God's Word, you remove trashy thoughts, resulting in comfort and peace. But if you allow the enemy to narrate your circumstances, you permit the decaying pile of garbage to grow, resulting in even more damage.

Rats prefer to invade at night, where they can't be seen. In the same way, the adversary likes to keep you unaware of his activities. When you resist him, bringing the truth into the light, he will flee (James 4.7).

Con Artist

Another metaphor of the pillaging deceiver is the con artist. One of my favorite movies is *The Sting*, which won the Academy Award for Best Picture in 1973. I found the plot twists amazing, the music spectacular, and the depression-era setting intriguing. Growing up, my grandmother told me stories about the hardships she faced during the Great Depression, so I have always found it interesting to know more about that time period.

The main characters in the movie (played by Robert Redford and Paul Newman) are confidence artists, commonly known as "con men." They made their living by designing elaborate schemes to draw people into their confidence, and then have the victims ("the mark") hand over their money voluntarily. Redford and Newman craft a scheme to entice a mob boss (played by Robert Shaw) to place a bet on a fake horse race. Working patiently and methodically, they win Shaw's confidence before closing the trap.

Con artists are still active today, using updated techniques. Most people have heard of the "ponzi scheme," where the con artist gets the mark to invest in a business that starts paying dividends. The con artist slowly siphons off the investment money, leaving the mark with no return and loss of the initial investment.

Perhaps the most well-known scheme used today is where the con artist sends an email, portraying herself as a distraught family member, caught overseas without funds. The con artist asks a grandmother or uncle to wire money to a foreign account that will presumably rescue the suffering family member. But the funds are actually routed to the con artist's bank account, never to be seen again.

Personalized Cons

Paul said to "put on the whole armor of God, that you may be able to stand against the *schemes* of the devil" and to "no longer be children, tossed to and fro by the waves and carried about by every wind of doctrine, by human cunning, by craftiness in deceitful *schemes*." (Eph. 6.11, 4.14). The word "schemes"refers to the craft of a con artist through a *fixed dice game*, a gambling scheme where the mark greedily pursues quick return. But the confidence man has weighted the dice to roll in a predictable pattern that benefits the con artist. The mark ends up voluntarily relinquishing his money to the con artist.

In the same way, we are instructed to be aware of the deceiver's schemes, his confidence artistry. He sizes us up and designs a targeted scheme, a personal con to rob us of our possessions. While God invests in a slow, long-term return on investment, the devil tries to trick us into "get-rich-quick" gambling schemes.

Since the deceiver cannot rob us at gunpoint, cannot harm us without God's permission, and cannot take away our salvation in Christ, the best he can do is trick us into voluntarily discarding our riches. He knows we have a rich inheritance through Jesus Christ that is untouchable by his hands. But he also knows that if he tricks us, we might voluntarily exchange our joy, confidence, or trust in God for short-term popularity, success, or pleasure.

So like a con artist he says, "Give me what you have and I'll give you double the happiness. Give up your wife and kids through an affair; you'll be happy. Give up your peace by worrying; life will be better. Give up your self-control through pornography; you'll escape loneliness. Give up your relationships by joining a faction; you will feel vindicated."

In all these examples, you won't get what was promised, and you will lose what little you already had. You end up with nothing. He wants to steal, kill, destroy, but by your own hand. He deceived Adam and Even to give up their blessings of their own accord. In the same way, he wants to dispossess you by abandoning your own fortune.

Christ has acquired priceless treasures for us. We have possessions! But Satan wants to see that we are separated from God's good gifts, causing us damage and regret in the process. The devil will use doubt, intimidation, temptation, division, harassment, confusion, and the element of surprise – anything that will be useful in a personalized scheme to harm ourselves.[18] He tailors the con depending on his mark, whether the person is a CEO, a prostitute, a pastor, a drug addict, or a suburban soccer mom. No one is exempt.

Pillaging in the Brain

The unseen pillaging by the adversary manifests itself in the physical world via *our brains*. A chaotic mind, filled with rogue thoughts of anxiety, worry, and fear sends a signal forming DNA in our brains. For example, those who suffer from post-traumatic stress disorder (PTSD) have experienced crushing events that altered their brain structure. During the trauma, the person reacted to the event in such a way that wired in toxic thoughts. As the person relives the event over and over, the wiring becomes increasingly permanent, producing flashbacks that reinforce destructive thoughts.[19]

The father of lies uses many schemes to wire in damaging strongholds in our brains. Like a rodent, he hunts for an opening for infestation, and like a con artist he designs a personal strategy to dispossess us. However, the Bible and the experience of saints through history expose the most common schemes used by the enemy. We do not need to be caught unaware. Instead, we can hear a message, stop, and *Think Again* about its meaning before being deceived.

THINK AGAIN

CHAPTER 4

Pillaging Schemes #1-6

Because there is one truth and thousands of lies, there is no possible way to exhaustively catalog every falsehood of the adversary. However, since the time of Adam and Eve, the deceiver has employed the same general pillaging formula found in Genesis 3.1-6: *"You will not surely die . . . for God knows that when you eat of it your eyes will be opened, and you will be like God, knowing good and evil."* Notice three deceptions ingredient to this formula:

1. God doesn't tell the truth (God is holding out on you).
2. You don't have everything you need (there are hidden things you need that you don't even know about).
3. It's up to you to obtain what you lack (God won't help so you are responsible for everything).

Satan constantly uses this template: you can't trust God; you are lacking something; it's up to you to make up for what is lacking. All his schemes touch on some form of this basic strategy, fearfully driving us toward instant gratification, public adoration, and power through wealth (and all without God's help).

The twelve pillaging schemes that follow are based on my personal observation, and they are not meant to be exhaustive or authoritative. In fact, you may have your own list.

Scheme #1: You Are Deficient

One of the accuser's principal methods of operation is to prompt you to focus on your deficiencies:

- I lack significance.
- I lack safety and security, especially for my loved ones.
- I am missing out on the pleasures of life.
- I am disappointed with my work.
- I lack friends.
- I lack recognition and admiration.
- I am too old, too young, under-qualified, or over-qualified.
- It's too late for me, it's too soon for me.

The enemy wants to focus your attention what you *don't* have, while God wants you to consider what you do have. If the deceiver can get you to fixate on what you lack, you take your eyes off God's good provision. If you choose thankfulness you neutralize the devil's temptations to be a victim. Instead of complaining and whining, you can learn to be content in all situations, whether facing plenty or want (Phil. 4.11-13). It takes discipline to choose thankfulness, resisting thoughts of deficiency, which is why thankfulness is a primary resource in spiritual warfare (Eph. 5.20).

One species of deficiency is fear of being left out. Perhaps Eve feared being left out of some inner circle, believing that God had a secret knowledge he was holding back from her. The devil got her to believe that if she ate of the fruit, she would be on the inside and not left out. The tragedy was, she was already on the inside and gained nothing through her rebellion.

One way you can recognize the deceiver's scheme of deficiency is when you experience condemning, harsh, and discouraging words. Satan asks to sift God's people like wheat (Luke 22.31), but God is gentle with us. The Spirit is merciful and encouraging, telling you, "Don't be afraid, it's OK, you can make it." Have you ever noticed that the smallest doubt, even the size of post-it note, can trump the weight of what the Bible says? If you ignore the Word of God, feelings of deficiency can quickly overwhelm you.

Scheme #2: The Answers Are Inside You

We have a tendency toward self-reflection (focusing on what's inside of us), making us dissatisfied with life. We are subjected to daily reminders of products that we need in order to be happy. This is one reason why we are a people that has become heavily dependent on anti-depressants. Our disposition toward the inner self (rather than outward truth about God) has made us weak and ineffective in spiritual warfare.

Conventional wisdom says, "You feel better when you are free to do whatever you want, without any consequences." On the contrary, studies show that when people live according to a strict code of moral conduct, with ramifications for their behavior, they are more hopeful, optimistic, and less likely to be depressed.[20] So many people suffer from emotional disorders because they lack a set of absolutes that exist outside of their personal experience. True identity is not based on how we feel inside, but is defined by Someone outside of ourselves.

Even Christian families can be affected by this scheme. From a young age people are conditioned to draw a circle around their personal preferences, evaluating every event as it relates to self.

The Christian life becomes "my personal relationship with Jesus," where everything is about "me and God." The Bible is reduced to "my personal handbook for living" and the local church is there to "meet my needs." God exists to provide a "wonderful plan for my life."

Gordon Fee said: "Both secular psychology and much Christian teaching focus on the inner self: How am I doing according to some set of criteria for wholeness? Focused on the inner struggle, we can scarcely see Christ or walk confidently in the way of the Spirit. Instead of living out the fruit of the Spirit, in constant thankfulness for what the Spirit is doing in our lives and in the lives of others, our individualistic faith turns sourly narcissistic – aware of our personal failures before God, frustrated at our imperfections, feigning the love, joy, peace, and gentleness we wish were real. Our turmoil crowds out openness to the Spirit himself. In such spiritual malaise God almost always gets the blame."[21]

Scheme #3: Temporary Amnesia

Another method Satan uses is "temporary amnesia." He wants you to forget who you are, even if it is just for a split second. Simba forgot he was the future king. Neo from *The Matrix* became confused about who he really was. The Prodigal Son lost track of his identity and found himself feeding at a pig trough. Pinocchio got sidetracked from his quest and wandered to Pleasure Island.

When you forget who you are, forgetting your mission, you can fall into all manner of foolishness and sin. In a moment, you release every anchor that made you stable, every authority that kept you secure. How many times have you done something and said, "That wasn't me!" The enemy wants you to forget who you are, even just for a moment.

You fight temporary amnesia by putting on the armor of God. Like Superman, Batman, Wonder Woman and Spider-Man, you put on your clothes to show your real identity. When you know your true identity, you live according to it, making you less prone to sin and foolishness. You can focus on your duty, your contribution to his Kingdom.

You may say, "All that superhero stuff is fine, but my plumbing won't work, my spouse hates me, and my kids are failing in school. None of my circumstances make me feel like a super hero of God." While the ordinary events of life can squash the wonder of your true identity, what you *feel* has nothing to do with who you are. Nothing can change what the Bible says about you. To be a super hero of God means to start with what God says, not what you feel inside.

Scheme #4: Your Past Dictates Your Future

Satan wants to define your identity, allowing him to frame the debate on his terms. In the movie *The Matrix*, the enemy agent interrogates Neo by leafing through Neo's file. With mocking tones, he refers to Neo by his old name, "Mr. Anderson," reminding him of his past.

This is what the accuser does to us. He opens a big dossier, and slowly leafs through our past, pointing out our failures. He tries to corner us, framing the debate about our shortcomings, sins, and folly. He is often calm, portraying the past in a cool, rational, objective manner. But regardless of how the argument is framed, it is still intended to steal, kill, and destroy. There is a reason he is called the Accuser (Rev. 12.10).

The truth is that you are NOT defined by your portfolio. Nothing in your past or present needs to define you: not your job, not your reputation, not your sins, not your mistakes, not the actions of others, not your sex, not your age, not your race, not your health. God can use you despite your past. He used Moses, despite the fact that he was a murdering fugitive in the desert. He used Paul, even though he persecuted the Church. God is not troubled by long delays and detours in your life. *Your identity is not defined by the accuser reading your file!*

Neo saw the Matrix for what it was: a world of deception where people walked around oblivious to the real world. Therefore, he was not affected by the interrogator looking at his dossier.

Your past does not dictate your future. In the same way, you don't have to be a victim of every thought that travels across your brain cells.

Scheme #5: Relax, Take a Day Off

One of the schemes he uses is to coax us into taking a day off from the battle. One way he does this is by convincing us the battle is temporary, that it can go away. But the moment we said "yes" to Christ, the fight began. We can't stop it, and we can't hope it will go away. C.S. Lewis said, "The problem of the Christian life comes the very moment you wake up. All your wishes and hopes rush at you like wild animals. The first job consists in shoving them back, in listening to that other voice, letting that larger, stronger, quieter life come flowing in."[22]

Another way the deceiver urges us to relax is to think that all the important events of life are coming in the *future*. So we let down our guard, thinking the "big game" is coming later. Like Luke Skywalker always looking to the horizon, we can miss the opportunities right in front of us. Chole said, "We have a tendency to assume that main is somewhere out there, not right here. So we treat today with less respect than we should, as though the current gift of time before us is simply a filler. In such an atmosphere, it is easy for us to rationalize indulging our appetites because today does not really count, or, we will deal with the issue later, or, it will not make a difference now anyway. All of which are blatant untruths. Today always counts."[23]

A third way to entice us to relax is by constructing a list of rules to follow. Rather than engaging in dynamic spiritual conflict that looks carefully at how we walk because the days are evil (Eph. 5.15-16), we can rigidly obey a list of do's and don'ts. If we think we can check off all our duties for the day, and then be satisfied for a job well done, we are falling victim to this scheme. List-making spirituality reveals how low we set the bar compared to God's standard.

If you think you can relax and take a day off, beware! You put yourself in a vulnerable position when you let your guard down. The adversary wants you to settle for lesser things, ignoring the Spirit's urging to pursue a life of adventure in Christ. He gets you to relax, settle in, take it easy, ignoring the passions he gave you for the Kingdom.

Scheme #6: Overreaction

We can over-react to circumstances and regret it later. When I was a boy, I was an avid UCLA basketball fan during the John Wooden championship years. Every game was tape-delayed and shown at midnight, and I would get permission to stay up late and watch the games. During UCLA's record-breaking winning streak that had extended to 88 games, they faced Notre Dame on national television. With under four minutes to go, UCLA led 70-59, but I watched in agony as Notre Dame went on a 12–0 run to win the game by one point, ending the historic streak. I ran out of the house and cried.

Certainly my love for UCLA basketball produced real sadness. But my reaction was not proportionate to the weight of the event. It was an over-reaction to the loss of a basketball winning streak.

In the same way, we can over-react to situations that take us emotionally away from more important pursuits.

We overreact when we "major on the minors" relative to theological differences, matters of conscience, or politics. We can be more interested in being "right" about everything, giving unimportant issues too much weight and intensity, causing division in the body.

The First Six Schemes

You are deficient. The answers are inside you. Forget who you are for a moment. Your past dictates your future. Relax, and take a day off. Overreact to minor events. These are some of the schemes the enemy uses to steal, kill, and destroy. The next chapter will describe the final six methods of the devil's pillaging, rounding out the list of 12 schemes.

THINK AGAIN

CHAPTER 5

Pillaging Schemes #7-12

In the last chapter, six pillaging schemes were described:

1. You Are Deficient
2. The Answers Are Inside You
3. Temporary Amnesia
4. Your Past Dictates Your Future
5. Relax, Take a Day Off
6. Overreaction

Here is another set of deceptions employed by the father of lies.

Scheme #7: You Deserve It

A fundamental American assumption is that "everyone who is good deserves a comfortable life." So when circumstances go badly, we tend to blame the victim. "She did something wrong that caused her stroke," or, "He must have been a terrible dad since his son got addicted to drugs." This creates a judgmental attitude toward others but also makes us vulnerable to the devil's lies about ourselves. The accuser says, "You did something wrong, and now God is punishing you." If you believe these lies, God gets the blame and you feel like a failure. The truth is that many problems have nothing to do with your actions, but are a result of the fall, the sins of others, or Satan's lies.

If you experience trauma, the adversary will often suggest that you blame yourself. For example, he may say, "This was your fault. You're ugly, gross, nasty, dirty, disgusting and unlovable." He delights when you suffer the pain of abuse, but he also wants a second victory by having you blame the abuse on yourself. Such ridiculous notions must be recognized for what they are: a lie from the pit of hell.

At the other extreme, the adversary can use the phrase "you deserve it" to bait you to do harmful things to yourself. He will whisper to you, "You've had such a hard day, you deserve a break. Go ahead and (smoke, drink, overeat, steal, look at pornography)."

In the movie *The Matrix*, the villains tempted Cypher to betray his comrades by telling Cypher he deserved a better life. Slowly gaining Cypher's confidence, the opposition appealed to the hardship he was facing by staying loyal to his compatriots. After giving into temptation, the enemy killed Cypher. He ended up with nothing.

Cypher is a picture of a scheme that starts small and gradually grows, according to James 1.14-15: "Each one is tempted when by his own evil desire he is dragged away and enticed. Then after desire has conceived, it gives birth to sin and sin when it is full-grown, gives birth to death." For Cypher, distraction started with a simple thought ("I deserve this"), then it was conceived into a thought pattern. After conception, it gave birth to a stronghold that took root deeply enough to lead even to death.

For us, this can be death of relationships, death of integrity, death of a testimony, even physical death. Whenever you hear the phrase "you deserve it," be aware. What starts innocently can end in devastation.

Scheme #8: The World's Methods for God's Purposes

We can be intent on achieving God' purposes but get fooled into using the worldly principles and methods. Abraham was promised offspring through his wife Sarah. When it didn't happen in his time frame, Abraham took it upon himself to bring the promise to fruition, by having a child through Sarah's servant, Hagar.

Satan tempted Jesus to demonstrate his glory by jumping off the temple (Matt. 4.5-7). The idea was to use a public relations ploy so people would recognize Jesus as Messiah. But for Jesus, the world's methods were not God's methods.

In a society that idolizes business methods, the pursuit of measurable outcomes can be a distraction in ministry. Pragmatism calls out like the Sirens in Greek mythology. In the Kingdom of God, we can work hard, do everything right, and still have unsatisfactory results. Sometimes the prophets were commanded to be faithful with no chance that the people would respond to their message. Regardless of our cleverness and good intentions, there is no guarantee for quantitative fruit. In fact, a fixation with measurable success can lead believers to chase after the latest fads, which quickly run their course and leave them discouraged.

In the spiritual realm, you cannot always see what is happening behind the scenes, so stay faithful to God's direction regardless of the numbers.

Scheme #9: Just Try Harder

The sport of Track and Field has been a part of my life through several generations. My grandfather competed at the University of Wyoming, and my uncle John Lilly was a world-class middle-distance runner and Oregon State roommate of the legendary Dick Fosbury (inventor of the Fosbury Flop). As a boy I attended many of his track meets, meeting the outstanding athletes of the era. From elementary school through my college years at Fresno State, I competed as a high jumper and decathlete. And then into the next generation, both of our sons competed as high school pole vaulters. As a result, I have watched hundreds of races over the years.

The story is told about a young runner and his exuberant mother. As the boy turned the corner down the back stretch, he was close to the leader but fading. Struggling with all his strength, he saw a runner pass him, then another, then another. The mother yelled out to her son, "Run faster! Run faster!" (as though the child had not considered exerting more effort). Finally, hearing his mother yelling to run faster for what seemed like the twentieth time, he came to a complete stop, turned to the stands, and shouted back at his mother, "Can't you see I'm running as fast as I can?" He coasted a few strides farther and then dropped out of the race altogether.

The accuser shouts at us like this mother, "Try harder, try harder!" Like the young runner, we try as hard as we can to do the right thing, hearing the same kind of discouraging instruction: just trust God more, just read your Bible more, just pray more. This advice is more often demoralizing than helpful. The enemy knows we are likely to give up when the admonishment is, "Try harder not to sin."

When you hear the words, "just try harder," be aware that it may be a scheme to have you to lose heart.

Scheme #10: It's Not That Bad

When we sin, we often attempt to justify our behavior. We slander someone, but say, "At least I didn't start the rumor."

We dwell on lustful thoughts but are comforted that we are not actually committing fornication. We entertain hateful resentment toward someone but think, "At least I am not punching the person with my fists."

We have an amazing capacity to discount our own sin and look down on others who seem more sinful by comparison. In prison culture, the incarcerated recognize a hierarchy of crimes, with sex offenses at the bottom of the list. We are most vulnerable to danger when we discount sins as "normal" because "everyone does it" or because "I'm only human."[24] This gives the enemy an opportunity to keep us from confessing our sins and receiving forgiveness. It allows us to be blinded with spiritual pride and makes us vulnerable to temptations.

Whenever you hear the scheme, "It's not that bad" let it be a reminder to confess your sins and receive his cleansing power, believing that you can gain victory over every transgression.

Scheme #11: Big Begets Big

We live in a celebrity culture built on assumptions about greatness, specifically that *bigger is better*. A related notion is that "big begets big." Believing that whatever makes a big first impression will leave a lasting impression, we trust in the spectacular event, the home run that makes a big splash.

However, it is a general rule that whatever grows quickly will also die quickly. That which grows slowly generally lives longer.[25] In the Kingdom, the imaginative steward takes what God provides and makes it grow slowly, over a long period of time. It is not the home run that produces lasting fruit, but the infield hit, followed by a bunt, a stolen base, and brought home by a sacrifice fly. In the world, big begets big, but in the Kingdom of God, *small begets big*. Jesus illustrates this principle in the parables of the leaven and mustard seed (Matt. 13.31-33). It is the slow and steady growth that produces lasting value.

Christians sometimes are deceived into believing that Christ's Kingdom is best advanced by a celebrity endorsement (the latest sports figure, actor, politician, or millionaire). We are tempted to show favoritism toward those in power, when we should be chastened by James 2.1-4: "My brothers and sisters, believers in our glorious Lord Jesus Christ must not show favoritism. Suppose a man comes into your meeting wearing a gold ring and fine clothes, and a poor man in filthy old clothes also comes in. If you show special attention to the man wearing fine clothes and say, 'Here's a good seat for you,' but say to the poor man, 'You stand there' or 'Sit on the floor by my feet,' have you not discriminated among yourselves and become judges with evil thoughts?"

Be watchful for schemes that promote worldly values where big begets big. Use the slow and steady approach that bears long-term fruit.

Scheme #12: Preservation

There is one particular scheme that is so subtle that it can easily be missed. It is the scheme of *preservation*.

Splits the Pie

Preservation is a zero-sum-game, where one person wins at the expense of the other. The world is seen as a pie to be split, where "I'll get mine so others don't take mine." People anxiously cling to what little they have, or attach themselves to those with wealth and power in order to get more pie. They compete for their slice of control, attention, or possessions, believing there is only "so much to go around." Preservation is nervous about ideas that threaten the status quo. "We could lose our pie, so let's not rock the boat."

Feels Trapped by Limits

Preservation defines life in terms of limitations: the heavens are closed, and the sky is like an inverted bowl trapping us in. People feel cooped up, living and dying in an existence where only the visible is real. Feeling enslaved, they believe they can never be free. Aldous Huxley observed, "Most men and women lead lives at the worst so painful, at the best so monotonous, poor and limited that the urge to escape, the longing to transcend themselves if only for a few moments, is and has always been one of the principal appetites of the soul."[26] And Thoreau lamented, "The mass of men lead lives of quiet desperation."[27]

Despises Mystery

Preservation demands clear solutions and despises mysteries. It doesn't believe in spiritual battles, in problems having a cosmic origin. Therefore, preservation has a great mind, but has no soul. It is absent bold leadership, heroic battles, or risky initiatives. In financial terms, preservation prefers safe accounting methods and balanced ledgers rather than bold, aggressive venture capital initiatives. Instead of investing in a risky return on investment, preservation takes what is given and hides it in the ground for safekeeping.

Protects Status Quo

Preservation desires to give the impression that the empire they control is universally accepted, everything is fine, the situation is hunky-dory, and they should retain their reign of power forever. But the people of God consistently push back against this kind of status quo because we live in a fallen world that needs to be set right. Life in this world is not as it should be – not even close. Change, and big change, needs to come. The status quo must be challenged and the empire exposed.

Thinks Like Bureaucrat

Preservation has a bureaucratic mentality. It is obsessed with things that are countable, that which can be quantified, measured, and objectively assessed. It believes every problem has a cause-and-effect solution. Preservation wants to analyze God, to explain him in manageable terms, to harness his power for personal gain. If God's actions can be predicted, they can be used for individual benefit, to appropriate his blessings. So preservation values central planners who produce predicted outcomes.

But no one can establish predictive models about God because he cannot be predicted. Preservation demands concrete answers, despises ambiguity, and struggles with imagination. When C. S. Lewis was unable to understand Christianity, Tolkien reportedly said: "Your inability to believe is primarily a failure of imagination."[28]

When you recognize the subtle scheme of preservation you can respond with imagination instead.

The Common Thread

In all these twelve schemes, Satan's purpose is the same: tempt you to voluntarily squander the benefits Christ gave you. The deceiver will employ anything to keep you from focus on Jesus: distrust God, take it upon yourself to obtain what you need, or practice self-destruction. Your life is full of spiritual enemies and schemes to distract you from your true identity. It is a world littered with tribulation, trials, and difficulty (an already/not-yet Kingdom).[29] But if you stop and *Think Again*, you can remember that not every thought in your head is true.

Conclusion to Part I: The Enemy Pillages

Your body cannot tell the difference between truth and lies, but only what you believe. As a result, you are constantly bombarded by confusing and devastating messages that if believed, result in destructive habits and strongholds. The accuser's arithmetic is based on subtraction, but you can resist his pillaging schemes to steal, kill, and destroy. So your job is to *believe truth, and disbelieve lies.*

Having lost you forever, the enemy now turns all his energy to distraction, to trick you into throwing away the treasures you received from God. He pivots from keeping you blinded to keeping you discouraged and dismayed. He put down his old weapons and picked up new ones. He acts as an infesting rodent and a devious con artist, designing a personalized plan of attack. He wants you give up your treasures voluntarily through various schemes, especially the subtle scheme of preservation.

On the other hand, Jesus offers abundant life! He wants to bless you personally, but also to the point of overflowing for the benefit of others. God's work is rooted in multiplication, so he wants a return on his investment in you. Between Satan's *pillaging* and God's *provision* is your *participation*. God uses you to carry on his work of sabotage, where the playing field is your mind. You have the privilege of being God's agent of victory over the devil.

You are not left helpless in this battle. Even though the adversary is constantly deceiving you, thanks be to God, you can learn to discern between truth and falsehood. You don't have to be victimized by the deceiver any more than I needed to believe there was a snake in the bed. You can face the problems of life by the flesh (which won't work), or you can conquer life's difficulties by employing God's weapons that have divine power.

You can learn to *Think Again*.

Part II: God Provides

I came that they may have life and have it abundantly.

John 10.10b

THINK AGAIN

CHAPTER 6

The Father's Philanthropy

In order to understand Jesus's words, "I came that they may have life and have it abundantly" it is vital to understand the unbounded goodness and generosity of the Father who sent him (John 7.28-29). He is a loving Father who encourages, exhorts, and charges his children (1 Thess. 1.11). He is a philanthropic parent who provides for us. Too often, our concept of the Father is out of sync with reality. If we fail to recognize the Father as lovable, radiant, happy, friendly, accessible, and totally competent, then we have the wrong image of the Father.[30] His overflowing love, mercy, and kindness flows from his character.

Our Source and Sustainer

The Father Almighty is sovereign over all, the source of all life, and the sustainer of all. His marvelous goodness is demonstrated in his attributes, perfect moral purity, absolute integrity, and unbounded love.[31] The Father shows concern for all creation, providing for every creature in a wondrously complex ecosystem where birds, fish, animals, and microorganisms flourish. The Father is gracious, offering his bounty to all people, whether they deserve it or not. He shows a special compassion toward the needy and broken. He is slow to anger and patient in exercising judgment. His kindness leads people to repentance and salvation (Rom. 2.4).

When we fail to trust the goodness and provision of the Father, our lives can be ruined. Upon the examination of the many moral failures of well-known people, what they have in common is the false assumption that "God has required me to take care of my own needs." When a person stops believing that God richly provides, resentment toward God is the inevitable outcome.[32] Therefore, the downfall of respected leaders is not rooted so much in a desire for sex or power, but a lack of trust in the Father's provision.

But you can trust in the Father's goodness! Despite whatever circumstances you face, Romans 8.35 reminds you that he is with you. Whether you face tribulation, distress, persecution, famine, nakedness, danger, or sword, no circumstances are beyond God's redemptive purposes. Despite the attacks of Satan, you can be certain that the Father's unmerited favor is sufficient for all that you will face (2 Cor. 12.9).

Created in His Image

The Father demonstrates his philanthropy through the adaptability found in his creation. God designed the amazing ability for life to adapt in a changing environment. This is especially true in the highest of his creation: humankind, the *imago dei*.

Recent scientific research in what is called "epigenetics" has shown how flexible God has made the human brain. Our brain is "neuroplastic," meaning it can change and grow.[33] The scientific community used to believe that once our brains were damaged, they could not be restored. But now, neuroscience has verified what Christians have known for years: we can be "transformed by the renewing of our minds" (Rom. 12.2).[34]

The human brain is made up of real, physical, electromagnetic, quantum, and chemical flow that switches groups of genes on or off in a positive or negative direction based on our choices and subsequent reactions. Since our bad reactions have been wired in by our choices, they can also be wired out.

Our DNA changes shape according to our beliefs. Thinking destructively wires in toxic DNA that damages the body and the mind. On the other hand, DNA codes can be reversed by thoughts of love, joy, appreciation, and gratitude.[35] Because we are made in the image of God, we can stand outside our feelings and exercise control over our response to stimuli. We can decide how to interpret the meaning of events and avoid being a victim of our circumstances.

Like a person looking in through a window, we can observe a traumatic event and cause its harmful effects to wither and die, replacing it with a healthy perspective based on God's truth. The substance of toxic memories in our brains can be weakened, replacing damaging mental events with the Word of God. Neurons that don't get enough attention start falling apart, destroying the emotion attached to the trauma. In their place, dopamine (which increases focus and attention) and serotonin (which increases feelings of peace and happiness) start flowing, leading to the formation of new brain connections.[36]

Despite what anyone says, you are not controlled by your heredity! Because of the Father's philanthropic design, you are not stuck being the person you are today. While the genes you inherited do give you a predisposition to certain behaviors, they are not your destiny! Your thoughts can change the structure of your brain at every level: molecular, genetic, cellular, electromagnetic, and even subatomic. The power of habits can be broken, because the Father has an interest in who you become. You can become a new person day by day!

The God of Imagination

The Father is also the God of imagination. The devil uses the scheme of pie-splitting preservation, resisting the Father's imagination. When preservation wants to split the pie, imagination makes *more pies*. Preservation wants to seize power, but imagination wants to empower others. Imagination sees a universe of mysterious unknowns yet to be revealed, of complexity and wonder, while preservation says "believe only what you can see and measure." Through the diversity of his creation, the Father's *imagination* is manifested everywhere we look.

The Father is free to act in creative, surprising ways. He provides rams stuck in thickets, makes axe heads float, and releases plagues that discredit the gods of Egypt. He sends his Son as a zygote in a Nazarene peasant girl, dispatching angels to visit shepherds, while saying nothing to experts in the Law parsing out texts in Jerusalem. He sends the Spirit to appear in tongues of fire at Pentecost and baffles religious leaders through uneducated apostles.

The Father is full of generosity, providing every good and perfect gift that humans have imagined. He delights in his creation and rejoices in us (Zeph. 3.17). His sovereign rule can be felt like warm ray of sunshine cracking through the curtains.

Dallas Willard said, "We should think that God leads a very interesting life, and that he is full of joy. Undoubtedly he is the most joyous being in the universe. The abundance of his love and generosity is inseparable from his infinite joy. All of the good and beautiful things from which we occasionally drink tiny droplets of soul-exhilarating joy, God continuously experiences in all their breadth and depth and richness."[37]

His Image in Us

The Father's imagination is revealed in our ability to show imagination. Because we are meant to be perpetually creative beings, he devised a world that is conducive to our creative imagination and innovation. His earth is fully equipped to handle humanity's creative nature. Because we are cut from the cloth of the Father's imaginative nature, we can stand on the plateau of an open plain and see an infinite set of possibilities, eternal vistas that might emerge before us.

We are free to move within *boundless situations*. The Father's goodness has no boundaries. It stretches out to the limitless.[38] The world sees in limits, in boundaries, in painting within the lines. But goodness has no limits because God is free to move without limits.

We can be deceived into thinking we live in a small space, not knowing there is a larger world of freedom outside our bubble. Like Desmond from *Lost*, we can choose a life of quiet isolation in a bunker, believing it is unsafe to go outside. The enemy can fool us into retreating into a provincial existence, thinking it is dangerous to explore all the adventure the Father offers. But the Father's philanthropy, seen in his creation, our ability to adapt, and the use of our imagination, provides what we need to press ahead.

Willard said, "The intention of God is that we should each become the kind of person whom he can set free in his universe, empowered to do what we want to do. Just as we desire and intend this, so far as possible, for our children and others we love, so God desires and intends it for his children."[39]

CHAPTER 7

The Son's Potential

The Father has been lavish in his philanthropic generosity to all people. But without the work of Jesus Christ to redeem creation, much of the Father's good gifts would not be experienced in this fallen world. The Father intends to restore the brokenness of creation through the Son. In Christ, the Kingdom of God has come!

In Him!

Paul's letter to the Ephesians is a marvelous expression of the Father's plan to restore his creation through the Lord Jesus Christ. He has revealed "to us the mystery of his will, according to his purpose, which he set forth in Christ as a plan for the fullness of time, to unite all things in him, things in heaven and things on earth" (Eph. 1. 9-10). Several other foundational themes of God's kingdom purposes are listed in chapters 1-3, which is akin to taking an inventory of all the marvelous riches we have in Christ!

Because of Jesus, we have swag (stuff we all get) including adoption, holiness, forgiveness, insight, intimacy, assurance, belonging, hope, power, meaning, creativity, individuality, community, and an inheritance. Paul reminds us that all of this is because of Jesus. Through frequent references to "in him," we are reminded that it is only by Christ's work that we possess such potential for fullness of life, ending in the crescendo: "To him be glory in the church and in Christ Jesus throughout all generations, forever and ever. Amen" (Eph. 3.21).

Reservoir of Potential

Jesus is like a vast reservoir of living water for a thirsty world. He said, "The water that I will give him will become in him a spring of water welling up to eternal life" (John 4.14). But without Christ's work of victory over the devil, there would be no reservoir for us to access.

- He was tempted and victorious.
- He triumphed in his healings, teachings, exorcisms.
- He lived a life of righteous example.
- He died, was buried, raised to life and has ascended to the throne.

From the fruit of his victories, he provides gifts so we can carry out his work (Eph. 4.7-12). He rules and reigns to provide a constant source of living water through us. We create, bless, protect, and serve as his nozzles to extinguish the fires of despair. We are the instruments that Christ chooses to use to dispense his grace.

Not for Us But for Others

Jesus won the spoils of victory over the devil and empowers us to continue his conquest. He transferred us from the domain of darkness into his Kingdom of light (Col. 1.13-14). And now through our baptism into Christ, we have confidence, because our efforts have eternal value in him. He paved the way for us to follow. His Great Commission (Matt. 28.18-20) is an expression of his authority, directing us to teach others to be obedient to his commands.

He invites us to be the continuation of his work by telling us to "be strong in the Lord and the strength of his might" (Eph. 6.10). Satan offers a yoke of slavery (Gal. 5.1), but Jesus offers a yoke that is easy and light (Matt. 11.30). Jesus outfits us to resist the enemy's theft, murder, and destruction by giving life in its fullness. But that fullness comes only through obedience and submission to Jesus's lordship, a willingness to be forged into his identity.

This abundant potential is not meant to be kept to ourselves. It is meant to be multiplied for the benefit of others. Prosperity teachers talk about blessing for personal consumption, but Jesus wants to bless others through us. We are God's workmanship, his creative expression, created for good works in Christ Jesus (Eph. 2.10), appointed to bear fruit on his behalf (John 15.1-8).

Paraphrasing C. S. Lewis, God wants creatures whose life will be qualitatively like Christ on a miniature scale, where each person exercises their will to conform to Jesus's identity. God wants not only servants, but sons and daughters. He wants a world full of beings united to him but still distinct. Jesus longs to reproduce his life all over the whole world, through people who would do even greater works than he did (John 14.12). In short, God wants to form us into little replicas of Jesus.[40]

Compassion for Others

One way we deliver the Son's potential is by showing gentleness toward others. Realizing that every single person on earth is victimized daily by the enemy's personalized schemes has caused me to see how unfairly critical I can be. I can look at someone else and determine how easy it would be to avoid their temptations. But as I do, I need to remember that my struggles are not difficult for them. Knowing that Satan's individualized schemes are designed to destabilize each person helps me to be less harsh towards the failings of others.

Rather than show compassion for people stuck in their own strongholds, we typically respond poorly to their pain in three awkward ways:[41]

- Retreat (avoid them, not knowing what to say)
- Refer (send them to a professional, feeling inadequate to know how to help)
- Reprove (criticize them or provide pat answers)

Because each believer is an ambassador of Christ, a priest of the Most High, there is a better way than *retreat, refer, or reprove*. Knowing there is good buried deep in every person, just waiting to be released, we can deliver Jesus's grace and healing. Instead of descending into their pit of despair with a scalpel and a scowl, you can shout out to the wounded person, "I am on my way down with a flashlight! Hold on, we can get out of this pit together! You are going to be fine!"

Instead of "retreat, refer, or reprove" we can *embrace, enlist, and release*. By delivering Jesus's living water, we can calmly *embrace* their pain, *enlist* ourselves to go through trials with them, and *release* them to their potential. Instead of wagging a finger saying, "Let me give you some advice" we can open our arms saying, "It's going to be ok, I believe in you."

Because of Jesus's potential, we offer hope, comfort, and encouragement to others confused by the accuser's lies and schemes. Even when we don't have all the answers, we can delight in others instead of recoiling in disgust. We can help other believers find their gifts and calling so they can be all they can be. Because Jesus is our source, we come with living water of deliverance and joy, not condemnation and fear.

No Limitations In Jesus

In the world, you are limited by your competencies: money, education, experience, power, and influence. In the Kingdom of Christ, you have unlimited potential. The world needs those in power, but in the Kingdom, Jesus can operate in anyone: the poor, those who mourn, the meek, those who hunger and thirst for righteousness, the merciful, the pure in heart, the peacemakers, and the persecuted. These are the kind of people God used in the Bible. These are the kind of people he uses today to produce a return on his investment.

If you feel pushed around and battered by the circumstances of life, you may be desperately looking to escape, living in constant fear that more bad things might happen. You may fear there are icebergs waiting to sink you. But because of Jesus's potential, you can become a person who experiences the difficulties of life while being unfazed by them. Your joy can come from an unchanging relationship with God and his faithfulness. You don't need perfect circumstances to be happy. You don't need to be appreciated by others to be content. You can be forged in such a way that you develop a hull that no iceberg can penetrate.

Jesus is our example. He appears to have walked unstressed and unhurried. His peaceful pace implies that he measured himself by a different criteria. It was not where he was going and how fast to get there, but whom he was following and how closely they walked together.[42]

In order to become effective vessels of living water, you have to be forged, crafted, shaped, conformed, and molded to be like him. In the flesh, you are like a scrapheap of metal. But you can be reshaped and forged into nozzles that deliver living water from the Christ-reservoir, offering refreshment to thirsty people in need. His life-giving potential can flow through you. Because of the Son's potential, given from the Father's philanthropic heart, you can bring refreshment to the world.

THINK AGAIN

CHAPTER 8

The Spirit's Power

The devil uses schemes to rob us of our treasures, through stealing, killing, and destroying. But God does just the opposite by richly providing for us. The Father is overflowing in his loving philanthropy. The Son has achieved the victory over the devil, creating abundant potential for us to do good. But God doesn't stop at philanthropy and potential. He also gives us power by the Holy Spirit! The Nicene Creed declares that the Spirit proceeds from the Father and Son. When people in the Bible were filled with the Spirit, it resulted in them *doing something*. They spoke, they acted, they protected, they defended. The Spirit initiates action, giving us power to get busy!

Look at the frequent references to the word "power" in describing the Spirit's work: "I pray that out of his glorious riches he may strengthen you with *power* through his Spirit in your inner being, so that Christ may dwell in your hearts through faith. And I pray that you, being rooted and established in love, may have *power*, together with all the Lord's holy people, to grasp how wide and long and high and deep is the love of Christ, and to know this love that surpasses knowledge-that you may be filled to the measure of all the fullness of God. Now to him who is able to do immeasurably more than all we ask or imagine, according to his *power* that is at work within us" (Eph. 3.16-20).

We are equipped to fight the enemy with power as the Spirit leads us into truth (John 16.13; 2 Thess. 2.13).

If we are to be forged into the image of Christ, we need power that is outside ourselves. Notice how the Holy Spirit's work is characterized by power, action, and truth:

- He gives us power, love, and self-control (2 Tim. 1.7)
- We received power when He came (Acts 1.8)
- He helps us in our weakness (Rom. 8.26)
- He gives us wisdom (Isa. 11.2)
- He gives us strength for battle (Isa. 28.6)
- He teaches us, reminding us what Jesus said (John 14.26)
- He refreshes us (John 7.38-39)
- He sets our minds on life and peace (Rom. 8.6)
- He has power to raise Jesus (and us) from the dead (Rom. 8.11)
- Walking in him we are free from obedience to the flesh (Gal. 5.16)
- He provides gifts so we can for serve (1 Cor. 13; Rom. 12; 1 Pet. 4)
- He provides weapons for our warfare (Eph. 6.10-20)
- He fills us with joy, thanksgiving, and mutual submission (Eph. 5.18-21)
- He is the guarantee of our future inheritance (Eph. 1.13-14; 4.30)

- He gives us insight and wisdom (Eph. 1.18, 3.4-6)
- He provides access to the Father (Eph. 2.18)
- He builds the body into a dwelling place for God (Eph. 2.22)
- He gives us capacity to take in knowledge (Eph. 3.16-19)
- He speaks to us through the Word (2 Pet. 1.21)
- He gives us wisdom leading to a harvest of righteousness (James 3.13-18)

In all these attributes, we are the beneficiary of his power, expressed in three important ways: Making Us One, Bridging the Gap, and Making a New Creation.

Making Us One
The Holy Spirit is the "Great Integrator," bringing various scattered people and factions into a single body of Christ. He builds the Temple of the Spirit, constantly adding members, disciplining, strengthening, gifting, comforting, and encouraging. The Spirit integrates the body to the Head (Eph. 2.15-16; 4.11-16; Col. 1.28).[43]

The Holy Spirit is constructing a Christ-centered, fully functioning body, with a diversity of operating members, characterized by Paul's words:

- Saints equipped for ministry
- A built-up body
- Unity of the faith
- Knowledge of the Son of God
- Spiritual maturity ("mature manhood" like Jesus)
- The measure of the stature of the fullness of the Head

- A process of growing up in every way into the Head
- A coordinated body with each part working properly
- A body building itself up on love

Like a great music conductor, he orchestrates the body of Christ to function in harmony, according to the creative vision of the Composer. He takes our various gifts and coordinates them together for functionality. Every counter action of the enemy is to disrupt this integration, to destroy the harmony of the orchestra.

The Spirit superintends the fourfold description of the Church found in the Nicene Creed: We believe in *one holy, catholic, apostolic* church.[44] The Church is *one* because he integrates the one body to the one Head. The Church is *holy* because it is the temple indwelt by the Spirit. The Church is *catholic* (universal) in that it includes people from every tongue, nation, tribe, and people, all invited by the Spirit to join. The Church is *apostolic* because he guides her into truth, preserving her from error through the apostles writings in the Bible. In all these actions, his intent is to make us one.

Forging identity is never meant to start and end with you individually. You play your part, but it is always for the benefit of the community. Any healing that you experience is primarily meant for the body's healing. Healing is for the community, and comes through the community. The Spirit's help will often come through the local church, through other believers.

Bridging the Gap

We tend to think about the gospel story as though it ended at Jesus's resurrection and ascension. But we need to remember that God's work continues with the Spirit's work at Pentecost. Between Jesus's departure (ascension) and his return (parousia), the Spirit superintends the work of Christ on earth. The Spirit bridges the gap as the "Ascension-Parousia Differential."[45] In this new role, the Spirit was publicly introduced to the world at Pentecost as the Third Person of the Trinity. It is on that day that the Spirit became the linkage between Christ's work on earth and the parousia, called "the last days."

The Spirit's dramatic appearance at Pentecost also began an intimate relationship between the Spirit and the Church. We live in the age of the Spirit. He is our constant companion to help us live in the *Already* (enjoying the foretaste of eternity), and the *Not-Yet* (enduring the sufferings of the present age). The Spirit helps us live in the tension of the "already/not-yet Kingdom."[46]

He gives us power to be a radically eschatological people, directing every thought and action in anticipation of Jesus's return. This gives us courage to persevere.[47] The Spirit is tangible evidence that the treasures of eternity are given to us right now AND a guarantee that he will see us through to completion. By animating, encouraging, and empowering us, he reminds us that the responsibilities of life don't fall on us alone. We cooperate with the Spirit because it is our destiny to be triumphant and valiant until Christ returns. We get busy because he motivates us to do God's work. In short, the Spirit helps us *do stuff*.

The New Creation

Another task of the Holy Spirit is to form new creation.[48] As the Creed says, "We believe in the Holy Spirit, the Lord and *life-giver*." He gives life. Jesus was conceived by a work of the Spirit, with the willing cooperation of Mary. In the same way, the Spirit impregnates the Church to do the works of God. He motivates, inspires, and directs, but only with our cooperation.

The Spirit is the "evidence" that we are the people of God.[49] After the Exodus, Israel was distinct among the nations by its identification with God through the Law of Moses. The Law was a visible emblem showing they belonged to God. Because the Law was given after their deliverance from Egypt, God demonstrated his salvation by grace from day one. The Law was a gift to help them function as the people of God, a visible evidence of his presence with them.

But now the Law has been replaced by the Spirit. He is the new evidence of our adoption as the people belonging to God. The Spirit replaced the Law as a better and more permanent gift. The Law was a good source of temporary guidance for the people of God (Ps. 19), but the Spirit is better in that we are given *power* to act, not just instruction on how to live.

Spiritual Warfare

The Spirit makes us one, bridges the gap, and forms new creation. He integrates us to the Head, making the whole body function together. He wants a mature body connected to Jesus, as agents of mercy in this fallen, not-yet world. This is what spiritual warfare is all about: resisting the devil's attempts to disrupt the integration of the body to the Head.

Spiritual warfare is not the high drama found in the movies, but the day-to-day grind of cooperating with the Spirit who gives us power to be forged into Christ. This power is not just an occasional burst of energy, but a supernatural ability to change at a molecular level, to become a transformed person. The Spirit of Truth leads us into the truth that makes us free (John 8.32, 14.16-17).

The Father's generous philanthropy, made accessible through the Son's potential, makes us well equipped. But the Spirit also offers high-octane power that can yield a healthy return on God's investment.

THINK AGAIN

CHAPTER 9

God as Venture Capitalist

A venture capitalist is an investor who provides money for those who want to start their own enterprise, but do not have enough capital to do so. In order to help an entrepreneur start a business, the venture capitalist gives out of her abundance, with the promise of sharing in the future profits of that venture. The television show *Shark Tank* illustrates how venture capital activities work, although it is sometimes far-fetched and a caricature of serious venture capitalism.

Blessing the World

People with wealth have a choice. They can spend their money now on things they enjoy, or they can invest it, hoping there will be even more money in the future. They delay their enjoyment for the moment in order to experience an increased return in the years to come. This is risky, because there is no guarantee that their original investment will exist in the future. They give up the benefits of money today, with no certainty anything will be there later. So venture capitalists look for talented people who are good at putting assets to good use.

They look for a steward who will use seed capital to hire employees, apply entrepreneurial skills, and put in long hours of hard work. Venture capitalists show patience and trust, sacrificing in the short term in order to secure more blessing in the future. If the investment goes bust, the wealthy person loses everything, so investors must have considerable confidence in the steward's potential.

By releasing venture capital to a steward, blessing cascades into the community. People are hired, goods are purchased, and new businesses get started (who then hire even more employees). Investors' sacrifices bring multiplication of benefit to a society. In the same way, God invests in us to multiply abundance of blessing for the world.

Fruitful Abundance

The teachings of the Bible reveal God's venture capitalist nature, making frequent reference to God's Kingdom in terms of multiplication of outcomes:

- Healthy trees bear good fruit (Matt. 7.17).
- A tree is known by its fruit (Matt. 12.33).
- Good soil produces 30, 60, 100 times the seed that started it (Matt. 13.23).
- An investment in a winepress carried the expectation of a profit (Matt. 21.33-41).
- A farmer planted a fig tree looking for a return (Luke 13.6-8).
- A grain of wheat falls and dies in order to multiply into more fruit (John 12.24).
- God prunes like a vinedresser in order to produce more fruit (John 15.2).

- He appointed us to bear fruit (John 15.16).
- Through Christ we should bear fruit for God (Rom. 7.4; Col. 1.10).
- The Spirit produces fruit (Gal. 5.22-23).
- We are to be filled with the fruit of righteousness (Phil. 1.11).
- He looks for a harvest of righteousness (James 3.17-18; Heb. 12.11).

God desires to make an investment that pays off far beyond what he puts in. In the Kingdom, the process of wealth creation is achieved through spiritual entrepreneurs, stewards who cleverly take what God provides to innovate, experiment, adjust, toil, assess, and innovate again.

This means a steward must constantly initiate creative ideas in complex situations, exploit opportunities quickly, adjust to discouraging setbacks, and all without any certainty of a successful outcome. What works one time may not work the next time. It is not a linear process and is not for the faint of heart, the risk-averse, or the cowardly. Those who wait for a sure thing will act too late. Stewardship requires courage, hard work, and optimism; it requires love, joy, peace, patience, kindness, goodness, faithfulness, gentleness, and self-control.

Parable of Venture Capital

Perhaps the clearest insight into God's venture capitalist purposes can be found in the Parable of the Talents (Matt. 25.14-30). In this story, a wealthy man prepares to depart on a long journey and calls three of his stewards together to make sure his wealth grows during his absence. To the first one he gives five talents (about 100 years of a laborer's wages). To the second, two talents were given (40 years of wages), and to the third one talent

(20 years of wages). The first two went to work to provide a return on the investor's money, but the third fearfully buried the money in the ground.

After a long time, the wealthy man returned to find that the first two had doubled his money, much to the delight of the venture capitalist. Commending each one, he promised to reward their work with even more responsibility and a share in the master's wealth. Investors are thrilled when their risk is turned to reward.

But the third steward said, "I knew you to be a hard man, reaping where you did not sow, and gathering where you scattered no seed, so I was afraid and I went and hid your talent in the ground. Here, you have what is yours." Jesus reveals God's venture capitalist nature by saying: "You wicked and slothful servant! You knew that I reap where I have not sown and gather where I scattered no seed? Then you ought to have invested my money with the bankers, and at my coming I should have received what was my own with interest." The master took the wasted talent and gave it to the one who had ten, casting the lazy servant into the outer darkness.

Joy or Frustration

The venture capitalist is especially frustrated by the cowardly steward who does nothing with the investment. The investor made the sacrifice of giving up money, when it could have been enjoyed. Then when he discovered that there was no return on his investment, not even a little from a bank account, it was seen as a monumental waste. The disappointment is twofold: "I could have enjoyed that money I gave you, and now there is nothing to show for it."

Jesus makes clear that God is generous in his provision, but that there is a clear expectation for you to multiply that initial investment. The Father's philanthropy, the Son's potential, and the Spirit's power are given by grace but with anticipation that you will *do something* with what you receive. He wants you to *use* the spiritual gifts you've been given. He wants you to *multiply* good works expressed as the "fruit of the Spirit." He wants you to replicate his love so that the body of Christ can be built up, integrated with the Head. He is not happy when he risks his capital and you do nothing with it but fearfully bury it in the ground.

God is the great venture capitalist. He made the ultimate investment when he sent the Son to teach us and give his life for us. To top it all off, he sent the Holy Spirit to empower us so we can yield a series of returns on his investment. He has great expectations to double, or triple his capital – even bring 100 times the initial return. He reaps where he doesn't sow. He gathers where he scattered no seed. He looks far and wide for those who will bring an ROI according to 2 Chronicles 16.9, "The eyes of the Lord run to and fro throughout the whole earth, to give strong support to those whose heart is blameless toward him."

Conclusion to Part II: God Provides

The devil employs schemes to have us forget who we are, dump our treasured possessions in Christ, and give up our faith in God. But we are not left powerless against those schemes. In fact the Bible teaches that "the weapons of our warfare have divine power" (2 Cor. 10.4) so that we can stand against the schemes of the devil (Eph. 6.10-20). Through the Father's philanthropy, the Son's potential, and the Spirit's power, we are well-equipped to engage the enemy's attempts to steal, kill, and destroy, yielding a return on God's venture capital investment.

How can you participate in God's provision to produce that ROI? Part III will answer that question.

THINK AGAIN

Part III: You Participate

We take every thought captive to obey Christ.

2 Corinthians 10.5

CHAPTER 10

The Difficulties of Life

The enemy pillages. He longs to dispossess you, discourage you, and tempt you to self-destructive behavior. His math is based on subtraction.

God provides. He desires to produce a return on his investment, overflowing in blessing and abundance for others. His math is based on multiplication.

On one side the enemy *pillages*; on the other side God *provides*. In the middle, you *participate* based on the choices you make.

Enemy Pillages **God Provides**
You Participate

God's provision is given so he can unleash our potential against the devil. He is looking to invest in daring people with daring plans, people who are willing to go where darkness reigns; people who are more afraid of missed opportunities than failure. Mark Batterson said, "I would like to think that when I pronounce the benediction at the end or our church services, I am sending dangerous people back into their natural habitat to wreak havoc on the Enemy."[50]

But most of the time we don't want daring adventures. We prefer stability and clarity. We resist a life of upheaval and disorientation. We find uncertainty frustrating. We want to know where we are going so we can exercise control over our lives. In fact, much of our prayers and efforts are focused on how to manage our circumstances, to keep our house in order. But God can use disorientation to start new trajectories in our lives, to re-orient us with new dependence on him.

Instead of controlling our circumstances, we need to put more effort into *taking control of our thinking*. We leave the doors of our minds wide open, allowing any stray idea to come in. Then when the idea runs rampant, we cry out to God to get the critter out of our house. The better strategy is to control unwanted entry, never allowing the pest into our minds in the first place.

Weapons of the Flesh

Paul says there are two ways to deal with the problems of life: 1) by the flesh or 2) with weapons having divine power. "For the weapons of our warfare are not of the flesh but have divine power to destroy strongholds" (2 Cor. 10.4). Dealing with life *by the flesh* is evident when we live as though everything is on our shoulders, believing we must be in control all the time. We act in our own strength, as if there were no God. We attempt to make life turn out the way we want, rather than simply doing what is right and trusting God with the results. We frantically manage our circumstances with gritted teeth and selfish determination.

This results in factions and divisions, in power struggles, in competing for influence and possessions (Gal. 5.19-21; James 3.14-16). In the end we are left with inferiority, insecurity, inadequacy, guilt, worry, and doubt. *By-the-flesh* living leaves us bitter, depressed, angry, hyper-sensitive, and distrustful.[51]

So we work hard, pursue degrees, and try to be famous so we will be loved and admired, but become *workaholics and narcissists.* We try to please everyone and avoid hurting their feelings so we will be cherished and appreciated, but become *co-dependent.* We demand to be in control of our environment and become *passive-aggressive.* We fight aging and death, becoming *obsessive* about our appearance, what we eat, and how much we exercise. We try to protect our families at all costs, and become *compulsive or paranoid.*

Waging war by the flesh is easy to spot: it is full of desperation, anxiety, and disorder. It is constantly scrambling and never at peace. Modern-day America is the most worry-prone culture in history, with 200 classified forms of mental illness.[52] We attempt to compensate for our fears with shopping, work, food, recreation, video games, drugs, achievements, and other addictions.

God loves us so much that he will frustrate our attempts to fight with weapons by the flesh. When we pursue adequacy on our own, he takes us through the *desert.* When we explore answers on our own, he allows us to experience *confusion.* When we seek security on our own, he allows us to go through *hard times.* When we secure pleasure on our own, he shows us the *destructiveness* of sin so we realize it's not as fun as we imagined. As we go through the desert, confusion, hard times, and destruction, he forges us into Christlikeness, providing we are willing to cooperate with him in the process.[53]

Weapons with Firepower

The weapons of the flesh are too weak to conquer the problems of life. We need weapons that have supernatural, divine power. We can pursue inner calm and poise by controlling our *outward circumstances* (by the flesh), or we can find inner calm and poise through *inward conditioning* (cooperating with the Spirit to forge our identity). We are no longer debtors to ineffective works by the flesh, but we now live according to the Spirit's forging power (Rom. 8.1-12).

By the flesh, we attempt to make life work on our own. We try to win the respect of people and find meaning in life. We investigate answers and implement plans. We ensure nothing bad happens to our loved ones. We try to make sure we attain what gives us pleasure. But our efforts to find adequacy, answers, security, and pleasure cannot be found through our effort. Forging identity means presenting our bodies as living sacrifices to the Spirit, in a repeated pattern of putting to death our bad habits and replacing them with Christlike ones. By the Spirit, we can put the flesh to death (Rom. 8.12-15).

Thanks be to God! He has a different strategy, providing weapons that really work. He forges you into the identity of Christ by making you strong on the inside, like our Lord Jesus. If you submit to the Spirit, he will show you how to experience true and lasting adequacy, answers, security, and pleasure that cannot be taken away by circumstances. The Bible tells us that the Spirit does this through three-dimensional forging: 1) *demolishing* strongholds of the past, 2) *detaining* lies of the present, and 3) *defending* against disobedience in the future.

THINK AGAIN

CHAPTER 11

3-D Forging: Demolish, Detain, Defend

God reveals how to be forged into the image of Christ:[54] *For the weapons of our warfare . . . have divine power to destroy strongholds. We destroy arguments and every lofty opinion raised against the knowledge of God, and take every thought captive to obey Christ, being ready to punish every disobedience, when your obedience is complete* (2 Cor. 10.4-6).

We have to *demolish* the strongholds that have built up in our brains over time. We also have to *detain* new lies that come at us in the present. Finally, we have be prepared to *defend* the ground already taken by punishing disobedience that comes back in the future.

Demolishing Strongholds of the Past

Strongholds have formed in your brain by the lies you have believed.[55] When ideas come at you (even as you read the words on the page before you), neurons form in your brain. It has been estimated that you have as many as 30,000 thoughts per day. These neurons cluster into branches called dendrites that become hardened over time. If you continue to reinforce these branches, after a few weeks of sustained belief, they grow and become permanent habits and attitudes.

What starts as a seemingly harmless lie, can grow into a permanent stronghold if you let it. When a lie is believed over several days, it becomes physiologically established in your brain, leading to anxiety, bitterness, and even mental or physical illness. So strongholds are formed in your brain by *what you believe*. For example, the enemy may tell you, "You're not a Christian, look at what you just did!" If you accept that lie, believing that God has rejected you, a pliable physical DNA structure forms in your brain at that very moment. Upon several encounters of believing that lie, it becomes a hardened branch in your brain.

After a few months of acceptance of lies, the stronghold becomes so automatic that you don't even think about it. Because Jesus said you speak out of the overflow of your heart (Luke 6.45), you begin to verbalize aspects of the deceptive stronghold without even noticing what you are saying. Negative talk starts spilling out in your conversation, planting seeds of lies in the brains of those who hear you, reproducing your poisonous thoughts in others.

Forging Metal

Praise God, strongholds can be destroyed and replaced with healthy brain structure, much like the process of forging metal. Metal is made up of microscopic crystal structures that must be crushed together in order to form a stronger crystal structure. The forging process starts with scrap metal . . .

. . . that is melted at 2500 degrees for several hours. Then it is poured into a large ingot that is pounded into shape . . .

. . . destroying the old crystal structures that are replaced by a new, stronger structure. It is reheated for twelve hours to make it soft enough to press into shape, and then is pounded again into the desired form and cooled down in liquid for six hours. Finally, the master craftsman shaves off the rust and forms the piece into the finished product.

Forging takes the existing molecules in scrap metal but re-forms their crystalline structure to make something new. In the same way, the Spirit takes who I am as Don Allsman, and forges me to be more like Christ. I am still Don Allsman and I don't lose my fundamental personality as an individual creation. I become restructured, re-crystallized, and re-wired in such a way that I retain my personhood, but become forged into the image of Jesus Christ. I am forged into who I was truly meant to be.

The perfection of Christ is combined with my inherent uniqueness, a person created in God's image. The result is a re-forged replica of Christ as Don Allsman.

Sustained Practice

The Spirit forges us into the image of Christ by pounding out lies and replacing them with truth. He takes the pile of scrap metal of your life and forges you into a nozzle that delivers living water to a thirsty world. You demolish strongholds by rejecting lies and replacing them with truth. This crushes the toxic crystal structures in your brain, and forms a new, stable structure in its place.

To demolish strongholds you need a few minutes each day of focused concentration on God's truth revealed in the Word. This can be done through prayer, worship, study, meditation, or singing, but you must practice this day after day if demolition is going to occur.

You demolish strongholds by observing the traffic of your thoughts, and then decide which ones can stay and which ones must be destroyed. Just as lies turn into branches in your brain, so truth can also form into branches based on what you believe. After three months of sustained belief in the truth, research shows that the structures crystallize so strongly that you can begin to affect others. You can disciple others, generating blessing that overflows from your life.

Detaining Lies of the Present

Besides demolishing strongholds of the past, you can take thoughts captive in the *present*. The best defense against a stronghold is to never allow it to take root. So when a toxic lie comes at you, you can choose to *detain* it by taking it captive. This allows the formation of life-giving structure in your brain. The toxic invader never has a chance to be established. By affirming the truth at that moment, God forges your identity into Christ's image.

Because you are created in the image of God, you have the ability to stand outside of your feelings and evaluate them. You can observe a feeling and cross-examine it, just like I did when Cathy told me I didn't have to put Clarence Thomas on the payroll. You can analyze a thought and decide to reject it. This means you are not a victim of your past. You can change at a biological level.

To take thoughts captive you have to interrogate them, asking, "Is that thought friend or foe?" Sometimes you need to say out loud: "That is a lie and I won't receive it!" Call a thought out of the darkness and force it to come into the light. Give the lie a name. Engage your thoughts and feelings. Don't let them rule over you. When Martin Luther was troubled by his thoughts, he was known to say out loud, "I am baptized!!" to remind himself that he belonged to Jesus Christ and was clothed in his righteousness.

The Enemy's Spin

Think about what happens when people say devastating things to you, like these:

- You will never amount to anything.
- Why can't you be more like your brother?
- We don't need you here, you're fired.
- I don't love you anymore.
- Your child has died.
- Your wife has cancer.

In that moment, the devil rushes in to whisper his interpretation of those words. He wants to put his spin on the situation. He wants to twist their meaning so he can steal, kill, or destroy. At that moment, you can choose what to believe: 1) Satan's deceptive interpretation, building a destructive stronghold; or 2) God's encouraging interpretation that leads to abundant life, taking the thought captive. For example:

- "You will never amount to anything." (No, I am somebody because the Holy Spirit indwells me and gives me gifts to serve his body).
- "Why can't you be more like your brother?" (I don't need to compare myself to my brother or sister or anyone).
- "We don't need you here, you're fired." (Yes, I have been fired from this job, but God has work for me to do elsewhere).
- "I don't love you anymore." (This person does not love me, but God loves me and wants to use me to bless others; he's not done with me).
- "Your child has died." (Yes, my child has died, but God will comfort me because he knows what it is to lose a child too).
- "Your wife has cancer." (Yes, my wife has cancer, but God will help me through it to bring glory to his name).

You are not defined by the accuser's meaning of these hurtful words. You are defined by *God's truth*. Like the security guard at a gate, you can detain a truck that appears to be carrying suspicious cargo. You can pull the truck to the side and investigate its contents before letting it inside the gates of your mind. Interrogate thoughts and feelings and refuse to give them access to your brain. As the sentry of your mind, you can take thoughts captive, refusing them entry. You can send them packing.

As you do this, you allow God's truth to dictate your feelings. By detaining toxic thoughts, you are forged into his identity.

Defending Against Disobedience in the Future

Just because you *demolish* strongholds of the past and *detain* lies of the present, it won't stop the devil from coming back with lies he used in the past. Because enemies will return, you must *defend* against vanquished foes. You need to be "*ready to punish every disobedience, when your obedience is complete*" (2 Cor. 10.6). When your obedience has been complete (you demolished past strongholds), you need to expect disobedience to come back and try to rule again.

Don't be caught off guard. You may think you have gained control over some stronghold, only to see it re-appear again some time later. The enemy doesn't like to give up ground and will try win it back. You have to keep taking those thoughts captive when they re-appear and not let the toxic tree take root again.

In the forging of metal, a metallurgist cannot leave parts alone and assume they will function without on-going maintenance. Without regular attention, metal parts fail when subjected to repeated use in a corrosive environment. In the same way, the adversary will not stay static. He will try to revisit areas where he once had stronghold. He will try to mount a return attack at a future time. Where you once gained victory over a stronghold, you will need to be ready to defend against return invasions.

Consider the example of Jesus's temptation. He was victorious over Satan by taking thoughts captive. He countered toxic lies with life-giving truth. But at the end of Jesus temptation, Luke 4.13 says, "The devil departed from Jesus until an *opportune time*." If the evil one would look for a later opportunity to tempt our Lord Jesus, you can expect him to do the same to you. Be ready to defend against future attack.

Hold Your Ground!

There is a hint of this idea of returning disobedience in Eph. 6.13: "Therefore take up the whole armor of God, that you may be able to withstand in the evil day, and *having done all, to stand firm.*" You are to first withstand in the evil day (detaining thoughts of the present), but "having done all, to stand firm" (defend another round). This is not a one-and-done process, but a repeated defense of what has been demolished and detained. You must *defend* the ground that has been taken, standing firm against future attack.

Larry Crabb said we need to shoot the adversary, "And if he doesn't stay dead, we must shoot him again, then beat him, then tie him down in the sand under a hot desert sun, turn loose an army of red ants on his body and walk away without sympathy. And then we must do it again and again and again, till we're home."[56]

Two Caveats

As you consider 3-D forging (demolish, detain, defend), remember that not every illness is the sick person's fault. In a fallen world, there are all kinds of genetically inherited diseases that are not caused by the patient's faulty beliefs. This is one of the main lessons from of Job: not all suffering and disease come from sin. If you blame the victim of disease for causing their own tribulation, you are in danger of collaborating with the father of lies, making the sufferer even more miserable. Be very careful not to assume cause and effect connections that may be more mysterious than you understand.

A second warning is that 3-D forging process will not be easy. Hebrews 12.11 says, "For the moment all discipline seems painful rather than pleasant, but later it yields the peaceful fruit of righteousness to those who have been trained by it." You must be willing to go through the pain. If you do, God will equip you to *demolish* strongholds of the past, *detain* thoughts of the present, and *defend* against vanquished foes of the future.

Demolish, detain, and defend. As you participate in the forging process, you will experience fullness, freedom, healing, trust, and forgiveness. As you Think Again, God will produce a return on his kingdom investment.

THINK AGAIN

CHAPTER 12

Two Participation Pitfalls

When it comes to your participation in 3-D forging (demolish, detain, defend), the key is distinguishing lies from truth. In the process of discerning between the two, there are two pitfalls worthy of special attention: *Awfulizing* and *Impulsiveness*.

Awfulizing

Awfulizing occurs when you tell yourself, "If that thing actually happened, it would wipe me out. It would be horrible, awful, terrible; the end of the world." It is taking potentially undesirable situations and blowing them out of proportion.[57]

For example, consider a young person so burdened with fears that she can't go out to find a job. She wants employment but says, "I've tried but I can't. I hate interviews. They scare me." When asked what scares her, she says, "They might look down on me and make me feel foolish. That would be terrible. It would be horrible." The truth is, it would not really be the end of the world if someone viewed her as foolish. It would be unpleasant, but not the end of the world. She is *awfulizing*.

There are two problems with awfulizing. First, the dreaded circumstances may never occur, so there is wasted anxiety over something that might not happen. Second, even if it does happen, it is rarely as bad as it was imagined to be.

Awfulizing is a self-inflicted source of anxiety. You fear things that probably won't happen, and even if the imagined fears come true, you inflate the impact on you. Although what you dread is unlikely to become reality, you may go so far as to believe that your fears are more than probable, they are *inevitable*. So you become a victim of your own imagination. The enemy has a field day generating troubling scenario after troubling scenario, watching you add fuel to the fire of his lies.

Here are some common lies of Satan to tempt people to awfulize:

- If I go out with my friends, they may laugh at me. That would be awful.
- I might not meet people's expectations and they would be disappointed. That would be awful.
- I might be rejected. That would be awful.
- I might make a mistake. That would be awful.
- I might say something dumb. That would be awful.
- Once I've gained happiness, I might lose it. That would be awful.
- I might not look as good as other people. That would be awful.
- They may not approve of me. That would be awful.
- She might discover what a nothing I really am. That would be awful.
- I might get hurt. That would be awful.
- I might be asked to do something I don't know how to do. That would be awful.

- I might lose what little I've gained. That would be awful.
- I could die. That would be awful.

Notice how many of these lies are connected to a concern about *what other people think*. Imagine if you could be free of the expectations of others. What freedom could you experience if you didn't have to consider everyone else's reactions to you? Instead of saying to yourself, "I need to do everything I can to prevent others from thinking badly about me because that would be awful," you could say, "What I fear may never happen, but even if it does, I won't like it, but I will be ok."

Don't collude with the devil through awfulizing.

Impulsiveness

Impulsiveness is at the other extreme. While awfulizing is a fear of something *bad that might happen*, impulsiveness is a fear of *missing out on something good*. Impulsiveness comes from a single lie: "What ever you want, you should have it, and you should have it *now*."

Rather than thinking through the wisdom of your situation, you foolishly rush ahead, believing you have to force events to happen. Physical satisfaction becomes the central impulse of your existence. She insults you, so you immediately insult her back. You have a bad day and grab food to feel better. You see something you want to buy and purchase it on the spot even when you don't have the money to pay for it. Impulsiveness is a reaction to circumstances without exercising self-control.

You can recognize impulsiveness when you believe that life is unfair. Waiting for something you want seems intolerable. If you experience pain or discomfort, you believe something has gone awry in the universe. You are fixated by entitlement, and constantly evaluate situations in terms of your *rights*. You react out of your own self-protection, and why not? As impulsiveness increases, thankfulness fades from your conversation and complaining becomes the norm.

You think your desires are too strong, and temptation is overwhelming. Out of desperation, you may ask God to simply exempt you from the rules of life so you can get what you want. This is what Satan offered Jesus at the temptation, which is called "putting the Lord to the test" (Matt. 4.7).

Impulsiveness is particularly debilitating because your lack of self-control can lead to extreme discouragement. When you fail at one thing, you notice failure at everything. You say, "I can't stop smoking." Then you notice, "I can't read my Bible." Before long, you cascade into despair, believing you are a failure at *everything*. You feel helpless. You want to gain control over your behavior but you feel no power to change. In the extreme, such discouragement has led people to give up their faith in God altogether.

Modern Families

Several decades of permissiveness in American society have promoted impulsiveness. Children learn at an early age that parents are eager spare their kids distress of any kind. So children are trained that the world should cater to them. As they grow up, they discover that not everyone bends to their desires so they are deceived by Satan, saying, "Everybody hates me. Nobody understands me. The whole world is rotten."

Rather than exercising self-control by learning to deny themselves, young people fall into all kinds of temptations. Discipline and chastity are believed to be impossible in today's world. Angry motorists become violent when their space is violated. Parents lose control at children's sporting events, verbally abusing referees, and shouting at other parents.

The Path to Victory

The deceiver has convinced millions of people that self-control is out of reach. Impulsive people bounce from one activity to another. They make resolutions, try drugs, surgery, or hypnosis to gain control over their lives, but sink deeper into despair when nothing changes. It is difficult to overcome impulsiveness by will power alone. But you can be changed from the inside out, by a work of the Spirit.

You can overcome impulsiveness by *replacing lies with truth.* For example:

- If I fail, it doesn't mean I will fail the next time; gaining self-control is a process, not an event.
- Regardless of the pain I've had in my life, indulging myself will not take away the pain.
- I can go on, even without that thing I so long for.
- Inconvenience, distress, discomfort, and difficulty are normal.
- I am in control of my reactions: I am not a victim of my feelings.
- I am primarily a spiritual being, not a sexual being.
- Denying myself doesn't mean I'm permanently losing a part of myself.
- Being mistreated and overlooked is the way Jesus lived.
- I am choosing this decision: nobody is to blame but myself.
- I am responsible for my reactions to everything.

To overcome impulsiveness, agree with these three truths: 1) I make my own choices; 2) I am responsible for my actions; 3) I accept the consequences of my actions. Instead of becoming a victim of circumstances, pay attention to those things you *can* control. Put less energy in that which you cannot control and more into what you *can* influence.

I once spoke with a ministry leader who complained about the shackles he felt under his leaders. I asked him to describe the aspects of ministry where he did have freedom to control. I then counseled him to innovate energetically in those areas where he possessed discretion, and stop fuming about everything else. Sometimes, you have more control over your environment than you recognize.

Perhaps the most important part of gaining victory over impulsiveness is to receive the grace of God and stop taking yourself so seriously. There is no condemnation to those who are in Christ Jesus (Rom. 8.1)! If you spend more time in thanksgiving and praise, and less time in introspection, ruminating over your failure, you might relax enough to be released from the grip of impulsiveness.[58]

The Better Approach

Awfulizing is over-reacting to something *bad* that may never happen. Impulsiveness is trying to make something *good* happen so you don't miss out. There is another way.

Think about life as a pure but unpredictable river. Impulsiveness launches a speedboat to outrun the current and rush toward the future. Awfulizing fearfully stands on the riverbank without even getting its feet wet. The better approach is simply to wade into the center of the water and let the current of God's presence set the pace, whether it is swift or still.[59]

Wade into the river and let the current of God's truth take you. That is how to avoid awfulizing and impulsiveness, producing a return on God's investment.

CHAPTER 13

The Practice of Forging: Getting the Raw Material

You may be saying, "All this is good advice in theory but how can I make this practical?" The next two chapters provide concrete steps for you to participate in God's transforming work.

I am not a trained counselor or therapist. I am a fellow sojourner attempting to let the Spirit forge my identity and produce a return on God's investment. I offer nothing more than a personal testimony. My approach is not the only way to do 3-D forging. You may choose a different way.[60] The weapons God gives us are the same, but people use his weapons in different ways.

The findings of epigenetics indicate that if you discipline yourself through deep meditative thinking, using different parts of your brain, you learn to capture and control your thoughts. As you pray, memorize Scripture, observe your thoughts, and think deeply about God's truth, you accelerate the brain's functioning, resulting in mental, physical, and spiritual health. This process destroys toxic brain structures and replaces them with life-giving truth.

Drawing from the practices of Dr. Caroline Leaf's book *Switch On Your Brain*, I engage in the daily challenges of spiritual warfare.[61]

Leaf's research in epigenetics suggests that it takes 21 days for certain protein changes to occur in the brain, so strongholds can be demolished at the end of those 21 days, employing practices requiring only 7-10 minutes per day.

After three successive rounds of 21 days (63 days), your nonconscious thinking begins controlling your conscious thinking, and you begin to automatically respond in a healthy new way. This gives you mastery to the extent that mentoring can occur. So 21 days of sustained forging can form Christlike habits, and after 63 days you can begin discipling others.

Dr. Leaf describes the following daily steps, each re-structuring a different part of the brain: Gather (become aware of your environment and thoughts); Focused Reflection (go deep with your thinking); Write (put your brain on paper); Revisit (create the change you want); Active Reach (do something). I studied these ideas and organized them in a way that made sense to me:

1. Pray Subordinately
2. Gather Subjectively
3. Focus Objectively
4. Write Playfully
5. Re-wire Decisively
6. Execute Repetitively

Pray Subordinately

Although every step of this process should be an opportunity for dialogue with God, *Pray Subordinately* forces you to stop at the beginning to subordinate your will to God's will. Ask the

Spirit to guide your thinking, leading you into truth. Put yourself on the forging block, inviting the Spirit to shape you into the image of Christ, like a metallurgist forming a brass nozzle from scrap metal.

Spend a moment considering the grandeur of his Kingdom, and your relatively small role in his giant plan for the ages. This will help you place the size of your problems in proper perspective. Ask God to remind you that all the answers in life are *outside* of your mind and body (the truth is not to be found within).

Sometimes this step can be done in a few seconds, and other times you may find it difficult to give God control of your life. *Pray Subordinately* until you can say, "yes" to God's will, no matter what it means. Give him a blank check, even it if takes a little time.

Gather Subjectively

The next step is to gather an inventory of your feelings. Sometimes people downplay their feelings because they know emotions can deceive them, leading them away from truth. But feelings are very important because they show you where your *beliefs* are hidden. Emotions are like a Geiger counter, revealing toxic beliefs that need to be re-forged. Uncovering your beliefs is important in the process of forging identity.

One time I took my car to Bob, our mechanic, when my "check engine" light came on. Bob looked at it the dashboard and told me, "I know how to fix that at no cost to you." Intrigued, I asked him to explain. He went to his office, pulled out a roll of black electrical tape, tore off a small piece, and covered the dashboard light so it was no longer visible. Bob's method of car repair is how many of us deal with our feelings.

Neil Anderson said, "Your emotions are to your soul what your physical feelings are to your body. Nobody in his or her right mind enjoys pain. If you didn't feel pain, you would be in danger of serous injury and infection. If you didn't feel anger, sorrow or joy, your soul would be in trouble. Emotions are God's indicators to let you know what is going on inside. They are neither good nor bad; they are amoral, just part of your humanity. Just as you respond to the warnings of physical pain, so you need to learn to respond to your emotional indicators."[62]

Encouragement from the Word

Throughout the Bible God encourages us to pour out our feelings to him. He is not shocked to hear our complaints, challenges, joys, and fears. The prophets and psalm writers express the rawest of emotions. As the Author of Scripture, the Spirit's inclusion of these examples demonstrate that he is not only tolerant of our emotions, but encourages us to express our deepest feelings.

I once did a quick study of the prophets and Psalms to find out how many passages began with expressions of grief or complaint, but concluded with praise to God. I found over thirty examples that followed the pattern: starting off emotionally scattered, but finishing with a mind fixed on God's truth. One clear example is from Habakkuk, "O Lord, how long shall I cry for help, and you will not hear? Or cry to you 'Violence!' and you will not save? Why do you make me see iniquity, and why do you idly look at wrong? Destruction and violence are before me; strife and contention arise. So the law is paralyzed, and justice never goes forth. For the wicked surround the righteous; so justice goes forth perverted" (Hab. 1.1-4).

By the end of the book, God has taken Habakkuk through a process that led him to see clearly beyond his initial feelings: "Though the fig tree should not blossom, nor fruit be on the vines, the produce of the olive fail and the fields yield no food, the flock be cut off from the fold and there be no herd in the stalls, yet I will rejoice in the Lord; I will take joy in the God of my salvation. God, the Lord, is my strength; he makes my feet like the deer's; he makes me tread on my high places" (Hab. 3.17-19). What begins with shattered emotion, ends with affirmation of truth. God clearly uses our feelings to lead us into truth, to forge his identity in us.

Feelings without Guilt

Some people teach that we should only say positive things, that verbalizing our fears will somehow cause them to happen. This is not the pattern of Scripture. Emotions are a blessing from the Lord because they uncover where the healing of God's word can be applied. The Spirit can encourage you in your weakness as you freely express your feelings without guilt.

You cause yourself harm by ignoring your feelings. When people say, "You shouldn't feel the way you do," it is a form of rejection.[63] God does not ignore our feelings and he requires us to respect the feelings of others when he says to "weep with those who weep" (Rom. 12.15). It is far better to give full inventory of your feelings than to ignore or suppress them. It is foolish to ignore a dashboard light indicator by covering it up with tape. So pay attention to your emotions, and encourage others to do the same.

Freeway Traffic Map

One way to think about *Gather Subjectively* is to visualize a traffic map shown on the television news or the Internet. Living in Los Angeles as I do requires frequent reference to the congestion of Southern California freeways. Some routes are red (slow traffic), some are yellow (less than normal speed), and others are green (normal speeds). A quick assessment of all the traffic situations informs an effective transportation strategy.

In the same way, *Gather Subjectively* is a way to list all the various feelings you are experiencing at that moment. Do not be organized or rational, simply list the various emotions you feel (sad, glad, mad, guilty, or scared). This can be written down or done in your head. For example:

- I'm worried about my daughter's grades.
- I'm happy about my project at work.
- I'm upset about my neighbor's fence falling down.
- I'm angry about Jim's offensive jokes at work.
- I'm guilty for losing my temper with my mother.

You don't need to evaluate these feelings, assign meaning to them, or counter them with truth. *Just inventory them*. Your feelings serve as an indicator of what you believe about the circumstances in your life. They help you evaluate where your mental energy is being applied at that moment. Your feelings are like a metal detector that identifies where your beliefs are buried.

After some reflection, you might discover some underlying ideas that you didn't see at the surface. For example:

- Nobody cares about me.
- I have no talent.
- I'm miserable.
- I'm lonely.
- I'm helpless.
- I'm nervous.
- I'm uninteresting.
- I'm no good.

- I can't lose weight.
- I can't control my passions.

Your emotions are like a thermometer; they register there is an underlying issue that needs attention. If you take your temperature and spike a fever, it shows that something is wrong in your body. Once you have done the work to take your temperature (*Gather Subjectively*), leave that list behind and shift your mind to *Focus Objectively*.

Focus Objectively

Focus Objectively is the opportunity to shift your brain into a different mode, to focus your mind toward what is objectively true. This is the part when you step back from your feelings and review the truths that apply to your situation. It is not time to interrogate or cross-examine your feelings (that will come later). This is when you list the truths about your situation, noting the facts like a dispassionate observer. *Focus Objectively* is where you draw from the fruit of past Bible study, memorization, and meditation. The Spirit will lead you into truth as you have invested in His Word.

Affirming Biblical Truth

Make a list of affirmations that declare the truth regardless of your feelings. While there are several hundred affirmations that could be drawn from godly wisdom (see Appendix 3, *Who Am I*), the following are some of the particularly helpful truths in my battles:

- His grace is sufficient in my weakness (2 Cor. 12.9).
- If I seek the Kingdom first, everything I need will be provided (Matt. 6.33).

- I have an enemy (1 Pet. 5.8).
- This is God's work, not mine (Matt. 9.38).
- I have everything I need for life and godliness (2 Pet. 1.3).
- People are not my enemies; every problem has a cosmic origin (Eph. 6.12).
- No circumstances are beyond redemption (Rom. 8.37-39).
- I have the power to be content in all situations (Phil. 4.11-13).
- Everything I have received is by grace, not my accomplishments (Eph. 2.8-10).
- God is more powerful than the devil (1 John 4.4).
- I am qualified to do his work (Col. 1.11-12; 2 Cor. 3.5).
- I walk by faith not by sight (2 Cor. 5.7).
- God loves me and has invested in me (Matt. 13).
- The Spirit leads me into truth (John 16.13).

If you have trouble coming up with objective truth, it may be helpful to pull out your list of feelings and then make a list of contrasting truths in another column. For example:

Instead of *(from Gather Subjectively)*	**You Can Affirm** *(Focus Objectively)*
Nobody cares about me	You like me and others do too
I have no talent	You have given me gifts to serve the body
I'm miserable	I can be content
I'm lonely	Thank you for my friends

Instead of *(from Gather Subjectively)*	**You Can Affirm** *(Focus Objectively)*
I'm helpless	You never leave or forsake me
I'm nervous	I can have peace that passes understanding
I'm uninteresting	I am unique
I'm no good	I have your righteousness in me
I can't control my passions	I am in control of my decisions

When you do this, don't feel the need to reconcile feelings to truth. This will come later. Your goal in this step is to assemble a list of truths.

Don't Explore the Root Cause

When you *Focus Objectively*, you do not have to analyze your history. You don't have to figure out how your beliefs went awry. You don't have to dig into your childhood. All you need to do is affirm the truth. Some thoughts and issues in your life are too deep to figure out. You can say like Catherine of Genoa, "I will not wear myself out seeking beyond what God wants me to know. Instead I will abide in peace with the understanding God has given me. And I will let this occupy my mind."[64]

Pray Subordinately, Gather Subjectively, and *Focus Objectively*: This is the hard work of mining the raw materials you need to craft a plan to forge identity. The next steps allow you to take the raw materials from this chapter and craft an action plan so you can yield a return on God's investment.

THINK AGAIN

CHAPTER 14

The Practice of Forging: Crafting the Plan

In the last chapter, the first three steps of my practice of forging identity were introduced: *Pray Subordinately, Gather Subjectively, Focus Objectively*. These steps produce an inventory of your feelings and corresponding truths. The final steps can help you cooperate with the Spirit by forming a proactive plan to produce an ROI: *Write Playfully, Re-wire Decisively,* and *Execute Repetitively*.

Write Playfully

Having *Gathered Subjectively* and *Focused Objectively*, now is the time to reconcile your feelings to the truth. Feelings need to be seen for what they are. They are not the litmus test for your reality. Emotions are *followers* by nature and you place your soul in danger when you let them take the lead. On the other hand, truth was *born to lead*. God's truth clears the fog in your mind, provides boundaries for your emotions, and allows you to make wise choices.[65]

You can know the truth in your head, but until your heart aligns with your head, you can feel confused and frustrated. It is difficult to accept the truth when your feelings are so strongly at odds with truth. This is called *cognitive dissonance*. For example, you say you believe that you are forgiven and that God delights in you, but in your heart, you may feel like you disappoint God and he simply tolerates you. You wish you could believe what the Bible says about his love for you, but instead you feel distant from God.

Write Playfully is the step that harmonizes the truth with your feelings, eliminating cognitive dissonance. This step is important because faith grows as you bring emotions into alignment with truth. Faith is having rock-solid confidence that what the Bible says is true. Faith is the perfect blending of truth and feelings. According to Heb. 11.1, faith is the assurance (feelings) of things hoped for (truth), the conviction (feelings) of things not seen (truth). If you have cognitive dissonance, you don't have faith. So it is important to wrestle through the step of *Write Playfully* until you comfortably reconcile feelings with truth.

Self-help Solutions

The self-help industry ignores cognitive dissonance by suggesting people can simply "visualize" or "verbalize" a desired outcome into existence. In other words, just "seeing it" or "saying it" will make it come true. The problem with this theory is that people may visualize and verbalize with all their heart, but deep down they don't really believe it will ever happen. Research shows the "see it-say it" approach often makes people feel worse when their dreams do not come to fruition.[66]

Part of the problem with this approach is that it leaves the Holy Spirit out of the equation, placing all the burden on you to visualize situations into existence. The way to overcome cognitive dissonance is to ask the Spirit to reconcile what you feel against what God says is true. Having uncovered your beliefs, you can cross-examine them, so lies can be put down. You can interrogate your feelings against Scripture. Regardless of how you feel, you can use truth like a thermostat, setting the temperature to control your reactions to situations. By affirming what the Bible says, you can bring your emotions into alignment with truth.

How to Write Playfully

Leaf's research shows that the best way to reconcile thoughts and feelings is through *writing* (using an old-fashioned pencil/pen and paper). Your brain chemistry is changed when you physically write your ideas because the vibration of the pencil on paper transforms your DNA.[67]

Your writing doesn't have to be limited to words and sentences (journal-style). You can be creative through sketching, doodling, making diagrams, using color or texture, drawing charts, writing a poem, or composing a song. The method you use for writing is not important. The purpose is to be playful, going back and forth between what you feel and what you know to be true, until you reconcile the two. You need to wrestle with your feelings until they come to peaceful rest under the authority of truth.

Examples

One way to *Write Playfully*, is to contrast a feeling (*Gather Subjectively*) to a related truth (*Focus Objectively*). Here are a few examples of feelings and corresponding truths:[68]

Feeling	Truth
It's terrible to have a husband like mine	He is my God-given husband and although I would prefer him to act differently, I can live with him without making continued demands that only go unmet anyway.
It's impossible to be happy with the wife I have.	It would be nice if she would change, but it is not essential for my personal happiness.

Feeling	Truth
I can't stand it any longer.	I can live a satisfactory and happy life even if he doesn't treat me as I want him to. My life can be fulfilling and enjoyable even if he never changes.
I'm wasting my life.	I'm not wasting my life. I'm believing in God to work in my wife's heart and make her the person he wants her to be. I am also believing God is working in my own heart, making me the person he wants me to be.

Once you list a feeling and a contrasting truth, write ideas that help you reconcile feelings to truth. *Write Playfully* can be a freeing experience, but it can be messy. Do not expect it to be a linear process. You may go back and forth several times before you reconcile your feelings to truth.

So-What?

If you find it difficult to *Write Playfully*, it can be helpful to use "so-what?" questions to get to the core issue, uncovering the lies you are believing. For example, you discover you are worried about your daughter's grades.

- Asking so-what?: "If my daughter fails in school, she won't get into a good university."
- Asking so-what?: "If she doesn't go to a good school, there may not be anyone to care for me in my old age."
- Asking so-what?: "If there is no one to care for me, I will die alone under a bridge somewhere."

The process of "so-what?" helps you recognize the absurdity of basing so much your destiny on a brief moment of difficulty at school. You can see that you are not trusting God for your life, and putting too much pressure on your daughter. *Write Playfully* can help you put events in perspective by identifying underlying lies, fears, pride, or irrational assumptions.

Expectations and Forgiveness

In *Write Playfully*, be especially mindful of the expectations of others. How much are you trying to impress others? What are you doing that is self-destructive that has nothing to do with God's view of you, but is important to friends, family, or the world at large? Is what you are doing ultimately important to God, to you, or to others?

Write Playfully can be a time to see others in a different way. As God reveals the way you need to be forged, let it be a reminder that no one is exempt from the enemy's schemes. As I have experienced God's forgiveness, he has gently reminded me to forgive others.

Re-wire Decisively

The next step is to move from *analyzing* your situation to developing a *plan of action*. You need to stop thinking, stop being a victim, and start taking aggressive action to control your thoughts. This is the time to be decisive as you re-wire the circuitry of your brain. Ask the Spirit, "What kind of person do you want me to become for your glory?" Then, take personal responsibility to put a strategy into motion.

Begin this step by developing a short slogan that represents the change in thinking God wants you to implement. You have spent time gathering feelings, focusing on truths, and reconciling by writing playfully. Now you need a concise phrase that summarizes what you should do. Here are some sample slogans I've used:

- I don't have to amaze anyone.

- Love, unify, speak truth.
- I have time to enjoy every good work.
- Seek the Kingdom first.
- I am not assigned to fix every problem.
- I don't have to participate in toxic drama.
- Content and thankful.
- Live on the truth-grace plateau.
- Waiting renews strength.

These slogans have deep meaning, because each one represents significant meditation assembled from the steps of forging: *Pray Subordinately*, *Gather Subjectively*, *Focus Objectively*, *Write Playfully*. There is much thought concentrated in a short slogan, capturing all the previous steps into one short, pithy phrase.

Execute Repetitively

Having developed a slogan, the next step of forging is to execute your plan. You do this by taking several opportunities during the day to stop what you are doing and *Think Again* about your slogan. Before you see permanent change in your brain chemistry, research shows that you need seven repetitions per day, for 21 days in a row.

So you need to stop what you are doing, and focus your mind on the slogan *seven times each day*. The repeated affirmation of truth is what God uses to forge your identity. It is interesting that Psalm 119.164 says, "Seven times a day I praise you for your righteous rules." Science is discovering what the Bible has already revealed: seven repetitions of truth forges you into his image.

For each of the seven repetitions, take a few seconds to clear your mind of everything else, and consider the slogan. At first this will be harder than it seems because your mind will be distracted by many other thoughts. But if you take at least ten seconds to discipline yourself by concentrating on the slogan, remembering all that it represents, the process will become more natural in time. You must stop multi-tasking and *Think Again* about the slogan, or the forging process will form new DNA structures in your brain.

Reviewing your slogan can be scheduled into your day in a variety of ways:

- Put it on a 3x5 card for review.
- Recite it in connection with a Bible verse.
- Put it to music.
- Incorporate it into walking or exercise.
- Review it in your quiet time.
- Put it on a bookmark where you can see it during fun reading time.
- Think about it during a TV commercial.

My Sample Schedule

I decided to fold these seven repetitions into existing events of my day so they were not an additional burden to my schedule.

1. When I open my eyes from sleep, I remember the slogan.
2. Morning devotion: I take a few minutes to go through the process of *Pray Subordinately, Gather Subjectively, Focus Objectively, Write Playfully,* and *Re-wire Decisively*. Sometimes this takes five minutes, other times longer as time permits.
3. At 10 AM, I review my Scripture memory and at the same time, I refer to my slogan as well.

4. While eating lunch, I remember my slogan.
5. At 3 PM I review a list of leadership affirmations, so I remember my slogan at the same time.
6. Going home from the office is another time to consider my slogan.
7. At bedtime, I have a reminder in my medicine cabinet to remember my slogan.

An Example from Chapter 2

Remember the story in Chapter 2 about my friend Paul, who asked me to consider giving up my office? Had I used this process I would have avoided much grief. First, had I started with *Pray Subordinately*, I would have allowed the Spirit to change my focus from myself, and I would be open to an opportunity for God to forge my character.

Next, had I used *Gather Subjectively* to list my feelings of disrespect, I would have detected the anger boiling inside of me. I may have noticed the pillaging scheme of the enemy to have me voluntarily discard my ministry over nothing.

Then, had I used *Focus Objectively*, listing the truth of the situation, I could have listed:

- Paul is a good friend and fellow warrior in ministry.
- Paul has not shown any history of disrespect up until now.
- There is an adversary who can deceive me.
- Every problem has a cosmic origin and is never what it seems on the surface.

- Division is one of the devil's schemes.
- Satan's end goal is to con me into throwing away what I have of my own volition.
- Even if there is disrespect, forgiveness is God's solution of choice.

Having clearly defined my feelings and the truth related to the matter, I could have used *Write Playfully*, to reconcile my feelings to the facts. Listing my feelings on one side and the truth on the other, God could have brought me to a place of recognizing my over-reaction. I would have been free to talk directly to Paul from a place of peace, giving Paul the benefit of the doubt based on past behavior, and with much less frustration.

Having done that, I could then discern how the Spirit wanted to use this situation to *Re-wire Decisively*, changing me at a biochemical level. Realizing that I was susceptible to jumping to conclusions rather than believing the best of people, I could have crafted the slogan: "Believe the best first." Then I could have utilized *Execute Repetitively*, repeating this slogan seven times a day for the next 21 days, reflecting on my earlier meditations.

Bringing the Process Together

The best way to develop good brain functioning is deep, intellectual meditation, using one kind of thinking at a time. In other words, *Gather Subjectively* in an intense way, then switch to a different type of thinking: *Focus Objectively*. After that, use yet another part of your brain as you *Write Playfully*. Turn your full attention to one thing at a time. That is how God designed us to yield a return on God's investment.

To do this well, you should avoid what Dr. Leaf calls "milkshake-multitasking."[69] When you shift your attention haphazardly from task to task, you don't focus your attention, resulting in shallowness, inability to make decisions, and passivity.

Notice how each step uses a different part of your brain and addresses different aspects of your whole person. *Pray Subordinately* addresses your ***will***. *Gather Subjectively* inventories your ***emotions***. *Focus Objectively* focuses your ***mind***. *Write Playfully* ***reconciles*** your emotions to your mind. *Re-wire Decisively* initiates a ***plan***. *Execute Repetitively* puts you in ***control*** so you are not a victim.

Eight Final Suggestions

1. When you attempt a process of forging, keep in mind that the real goal is to cooperate with the Spirit to make you more like Jesus, not for you to become well-adjusted or self-actuated. So don't develop a formula or method but relate to God personally and intimately. Play your part: He forges,

you believe. Don't be rigid or legalistic. Make the process work in a way that is natural for you in relationship with him.

2. As you demolish strongholds, remember to defend against return offenders. As you gain victory, don't be surprised when old thoughts come back. Sometimes I have needed to stop using my current slogan, returning to an old one so I can fight an old battle again. Don't be surprised when toxic thoughts return. Remember forging is 3-D: *demolish* strongholds (past), *detain* thoughts (present), and *defend* against disobedience that returns (future).
3. This practice is not meant to *replace* spiritual disciplines, but rather *assumes* you are regularly reading the Word, praying, serving in a local church, etc. For some references on spiritual disciplines see Appendix 4.
4. Remember, it takes 21 days of persistent work before you can get lasting change in brain chemistry. It takes three rounds of 21 days (63 days) before you have gained mastery and can disciple others. Leaf's research shows that people do well for the first few days, and then it becomes difficult and most people get discouraged and give up.[70] Stay with the process, trusting God to forge you into his image. If all this feels overwhelming and you don't know how to proceed, consider the ideas in Appendix 5 to get you moving again.
5. Don't be discouraged if you feel the need to change the wording of your slogan in the middle of the 21 days. Sometimes the Spirit has taken me deeper into the same issue and given me a different slogan within the same general theme. For example, I have started with the slogan, "waiting renews strength" and then a few days later I changed it to "enjoy future restoration." Rejoicing in the midst of waiting is the consistent theme, but as I moved through the 21 days, a richer and more meaningful slogan has sometimes emerged.

6. I explain this process as an individual exercise, but you can easily follow these same steps in conversation with a friend. If doing this alone seems difficult, ask someone to help you. The one exception is the step to *Write Playfully*, where you must put pencil to paper, reconciling your feelings to truth. However, even in *Write Playfully*, feel free to share your writing with someone who can give feedback on your ideas.
7. Many approaches to mental health focus on finding the source of the difficulty. While this may be helpful in some cases, spend your time and effort discovering truth and latching on to it. You can waste a lot of time trying to find the source of lies and never get to the truth. It is the truth that sets you free.
8. Some situations are complex and may require professional help. Some may even have a biochemical source. The ideas in this book are not intended to discourage counseling or avoid medication. Do not let the enemy accuse you of failure if you obtain professional assistance.

Pray Subordinately, Gather Subjectively, Focus Objectively, Write Playfully, Re-wire Decisively, and *Execute Repetitively*. This process has helped me to *Think Again*, doing the work of spiritual warfare: demolishing, detaining, and defending against the devil's pillaging work. The next section will help you apply this forging work to produce a return on God's investment.

THINK AGAIN

CHAPTER 15
Producing God's ROI: Adapt to Win

Having worked to *demolish* strongholds, *detain* lies, and *defend* against disobedience, you are in a good position to yield an abundant return on investment for God. Your mind can be released to creative avenues of service that focus on others and not yourself. But to do so, you need a mind-set that constantly adapts to dynamic circumstances. *You must adapt to win.*

Since the adversary adapts, so must you. The devil doesn't sit still or remain static. You are warned not to be surprised by painful trials (1 Pet. 4.12), so you must adapt by changing your approach under opposition and fluctuating conditions. Without adaptability, you will waste time and money, and be susceptible to anxiety and despair. With adaptability, you can stay fresh for the long haul and prevent burnout.

Life is uncertain and mysterious. Rationalism explains only so much. You can stay sharp and alert if you don't over-analyze every situation. Even bad circumstances can be redemptive; opposition can mean you are on the right track. Innovation can emerge from challenging circumstances, because "necessity is the mother of invention."

On the other hand, good circumstances can be deceiving. When everything is working you stop adapting. You fall back into old practices, thinking they are the reason for success. The enemy might even leave you alone, granting you paltry achievement in order to keep you from greater fruit. You can fall into pride, thinking you are the reason for your own triumph.

To become more adaptable, you must be willing to develop two skills: 1) *embrace obscurity* and 2) *cultivate your imagination*.

Embrace Obscurity

The biggest obstacle to adaptability is the desire to *win the approval of people*. Throughout the history of human civilization, we have dedicated most of our physical and emotional energy to taking credit and avoiding blame, maximizing pleasure and minimizing pain. We devote ourselves to appearing right in others' eyes, hiding our inadequacies, and promoting our success.

No one escapes this temptation. The gang-banger running the streets wants to impress his posse. The college professor covets approval from other academics. Each one wants to stand out among their peers. Each one desires the recognition that feels necessary for happiness. We all pursue the esteem of our little crowd, even though we differ on how to achieve that respect.

Like people on an airplane whose only pilot has died, we desperately look to others for assurance that we are OK. When we are petrified by this kind of insecurity, our minds aren't free enough to adapt. All our energy is wasted on getting approval. Living for admiration depletes all our ability to innovate, and leads only to despair.

Created to Be Significant

Embracing obscurity is challenging and counter-intuitive, because we are created by God to be significant. The impulse to be important is not evil. On the contrary, it is a quality embedded in us by God himself. We are wired to be creative, to do things that *matter*, to be noticed and appreciated. We are built to be indispensable.

But the devil takes advantage of this desire, hoping we will put all our effort into securing the approval of others. In a fallen world, the God-given drive to be significant can be twisted into an obsession to win approval or become famous. Wondering if we really count, we can become terrified of being worthless. So we frantically pour ourselves into activities to address our fear of insignificance.

Children will do anything to avoid obscurity, even act self-destructively. All through life, we desperately act in ways that we can be noticed, respected, and honored. We are warned by James 4.2-3: "You desire but do not have, so you kill. You covet but you cannot get what you want, so you quarrel and fight. You do not have because you do not ask God. When you ask, you do not receive, because you ask with wrong motives, that you may spend what you get on your pleasures." We have wrong motives because we want to be noticed, no matter the cost.

Do you find yourself inserting your way into every conversation? Do you find yourself wounded when your contribution isn't recognized? Can a discussion start and end without you becoming the topic? Or do you find yourself thinking thoughts like:

- If I win that award, they will finally respect me.
- If I can get my article published, then I'll be somebody.
- If I earn that promotion, I will have arrived.

You also need to be on guard against envy. If you become envious of others' success, you can become like Cain who murdered his brother. James said, "If you harbor bitter envy and selfish ambition in your hearts do not boast about it or deny the truth. Where you have envy and selfish ambition you will find disorder and every evil practice" (James 3.14-16).

You may even find yourself pushing your way into roles that put you at risk before you are ready. Chole said, "Over the decades, I have witnessed with tears the collapse of truly exceptional men and women who were crushed by the premature, combined weight of too much applause, too much authority, and too little self-control. So when I see those I mentor rushing toward the future or longing to be noticed or hungry for responsibility, I breathe a silent prayer: Oh, Jesus, grant them the gift of hiddenness. For a few more years, please let them grow in quiet anonymity."[71]

More than Humility

Embracing obscurity is more than just a casual attempt to be more humble. It is a willingness to be invisible or anonymous, like Jesus. Embracing obscurity puts you in a position to be forged. Your source of pleasure can switch from "the approval of people" to "the approval of God." The Spirit can demolish the strongholds of people-pleasing and replace it with new DNA in your brain that enjoys pleasing God.

In the seasons when no one is clapping for you, when you feel underestimated, unappreciated, or minimized, God can forge you. In the painful silence of these moments you have the opportunity to wrestle with what makes you truly significant. When no one is there to tell you why you are so valuable, you are left to look at Jesus and answer that question yourself.[72]

If you embrace obscurity, you will be liberated to put your energy into the task God wants to give you. In *Mission Impossible: Ghost Protocol*, Ethan (Tom Cruise) is wrongly accused of blowing up the Kremlin. The government has disavowed Ethan's team. No one will recognize their existence. At that moment, they faced a decision: would they embrace obscurity for sake of completing the mission, or would they walk away to protect themselves?

Embracing obscurity brings you to that same crossroad: If you proceed, it means getting no credit and no notoriety. You may be overlooked, disregarded, and given no recognition for past performance, education, achievements, or experience. At this fork in the road you can *go left*, becoming resentful, cynical, and bitter; or you can *go right*, submitting to obscurity that leads to freedom. When you face this kind of obscurity, your real motives come out. When nothing is left for you but the mission, can you embrace obscurity?

If so, your imagination becomes free for the mission. But if you insist on receiving credit in order to build your reputation, you reduce the number of creative options before you. There's only so much bandwidth available to make decisions, and the more you think about yourself, the less attention you give to task before you. You sever your mind from the unlimited universe of imaginative options. Only when you embrace obscurity can you release your full attention to yield a return on God's investment.

Condition 1: You are Adequately Loved

The first condition of embracing obscurity is coming to the conclusion that you are adequately loved by God. This is more than a theological acknowledgment of God's character. It must be a heartfelt, rock-solid conviction that God loves you and is *pulling for you*. God's adoring eyes have always been upon you. You had his attention all along, but you couldn't see it because you have been too distracted by the sight of yourself.[73]

You must be certain that 2 Peter 1.3 is true: "You have been given everything you need for life and godliness." This means you can walk in safety and security, confident of God's work in human history. You can breathe a sigh of relief because you *do* matter. You *are* significant. You don't have to earn others' acceptance, because in Christ you are already accepted. *You belong!*

Many people are incapacitated because they cannot accept God's forgiveness. You may live in a constant state of guilt and bondage because you don't really believe that Christ's blood is sufficient to cover your sins. But if you have confidence that God in Christ has paid the price for all wrong-doing, you can confess it, receive forgiveness, and quickly move on (1 John 1.9). He didn't go to the cross grudgingly, but willingly.

Knowing you are loved frees you to live a risk-taking, adventuresome life. The reward is worth the risk. Your labor in the Lord is not in vain (1 Cor. 15.58). You are safe in the proven love of God, the sure word of Scripture. God never leaves you or forsakes you (Heb. 13.5). He does not leave you as an orphan (John 14.8). Because God has eliminated the risk, you are set free to pursue the heroic efforts of any enterprise he assigns to you.[74]

Condition 2: Boring and Thankless Tasks

The second condition to embracing obscurity is an eagerness to do boring and thankless tasks. Most people consider themselves above the gritty and relentless details, so they are unwilling to pursue what seems "beneath them." They say, "I didn't do four years of college to do that." God resists the proud but gives grace to the humble (James 4.6). What if your purpose is to empower someone else to receive the credit? Can you eagerly embrace that kind of obscurity?

You may have a death grip on that which defines you: work, family, sexuality, reputation, or ministry. Tozer said, "We need to have taken from our dying hand the shadow scepter with which we fancy we rule the world."[75] Maybe you don't want to rule the world, but to let go of the scepter that controls your identity is met with a firm, "Over my dead body!" Embracing obscurity means releasing whatever has made you well known up to this point.

Condition 3: Releasing Bitterness

The third condition of embracing obscurity is to forgive others and not see them as enemies. When you refuse to forgive others, your mind is enslaved to bitterness. This is why Jesus taught us to pray that God would forgive us our sins as we forgive those who sin against us (Matt. 6.12). If you believe that others are blocking your potential or stifling your goals, you can lose sight that God is still in control. You may think, "My leaders are shortsighted, my parents don't understand, my boss is jealous, my spouse is dragging me down. The old-timers at work shut down new ideas, and the young people don't respect the wisdom of elders. The board is out of touch, and the task force is misguided."

Is the Lord really so weak that he can't overcome these challenges? Is he unaware of your frustration? Is he asleep on the job? Without question, you are affected by the decisions of others, but they are not the ones holding you back. There is only one person who can destroy your future. *That person is you.* You are the only one who can sabotage your potential by nurturing a bitter spirit.[76] You can decide to joyfully trust God in spite of your frustration.

Embracing obscurity is to rest in his love, take on boring and thankless tasks, and release bitterness. Embracing obscurity is to take up your cross, as Jesus commanded (Matt. 16.24). The way of Jesus is obscurity first, exaltation second. Good-Friday crucifixion comes first, Easter-Sunday resurrection comes later. The obscurity of the cross was Jesus's way, and the way for you too.

When you sow in obscurity, you will reap in recognition. When you humble yourself under God's mighty hand, he will lift you up at the proper time. He himself will restore, strengthen, establish, and confirm you (1 Pet. 5.6-10).

Adaptability is required to produce an ROI for God. The first skill that is needed to become adaptable is to embrace obscurity. The second is to *cultivate your imagination*.

THINK AGAIN

CHAPTER 16

Maximizing God's ROI: Cultivate Your Imagination

If you can embrace obscurity, you are ready for the next skill: cultivate your imagination for his Kingdom. God's way to create wealth is through the imagination and grit of heroic and sacrificial stewards, not by textbooks or wooden paradigms. Innovations cannot be planned or predicted because they emerge from the daring entrepreneur.

In business, the imagination of Steve Jobs (Apple), Mark Zuckerberg (Facebook), or Sam Walton (Walmart) has been widely reported. In sports, fans marveled at the ingenuity of Michael Jordan (basketball) and Bill Belichick (football). In the Kingdom, imagination has been displayed by Bill Bright, Martin Luther King, and John Wesley. God's design is to realize his venture capital return through your life. When your imagination is unleashed, you have the ability to innovate, seizing opportunities as they arise.

Buying Up Opportunities

Ephesians 5.15-16 says, "Look carefully then how you walk, not as unwise but as wise, *making the best use of the time*. The phrase "making the best use of the time" means to "buy up opportunities," which comes from the world of sailing (Latin for "toward the port"). The idea is that you need to be constantly aware of the winds and tides that shift one way or another, taking advantage of them to guide you toward the port.

To be wise is to recognize the winds and tides are more favorable at one time than another. So wisdom sometimes involves *waiting*. Other times it means *acting quickly*. I loved playing basketball because it is a game of constantly looking for opportunities. The best players make instantaneous decisions to pass, shoot, dribble, cut, or drive, depending on what is available. Even when a player doesn't have possession of the ball, she is constantly observing the situation to take advantage of opportunities that present themselves.

When Paul talks about opportunities, he prays God will open doors so that he will take proper advantage of them. "Pray also for us, that God may open to us a door for the word, to declare the mystery of Christ, on account of which I am in prison – that I may make it clear, which is how I ought to speak. Walk in wisdom toward outsiders, making the best use of the time" (Col. 4.3-4).

You must be continually ready for opportunities, especially when you are experiencing trials. When my mother passed away and we were in the midst of our own grief, we had to break the news of her death to several of her friends. Many of them burst into tears, needing words of comfort and encouragement. Out of the grace God gave us, we were able to be the source of strength to others. To recognize opportunities, you must be aware of your surroundings. It is easy to drift through life like sleepwalkers and miss opportunities.

You also need to cultivate your imagination in surprising situations. In *Mission Impossible: Ghost Protocol*, Ethan wakes up to find himself in a Russian hospital bed. Waiting outside his room is a Russian agent ready to interrogate him. Without delay, Ethan uses his imagination. He steps out on the window ledge, high above the street, and assesses his options. Suddenly, as a truck appears below, he uses his belt to slide down a wire, lands on top of the passing truck, jumps off, and secures his escape through a crowd.

Like Ethan, you need to use your imagination in difficult and confusing situations. Ethan assessed the surroundings using the resources available and crafted an ingenious approach. You can learn to do the same. God has given you resources but you need the imagination to recognize them.

One way to cultivate your imagination is to recognize and reject *preservation*.

Replace Preservation with Imagination

Preservation is one of the devil's schemes (mentioned in chapter 5), where the world is seen as a pie to be split, and each person contends to keep his share of the pie. Preservation attempts to analyze God and define him using manageable terms. Preservation prefers situations that can be tamed, controlled, domesticated, seized, entrenched, exploited, and conquered. Preservation desires rules, security, self-protection, bean-counting, and bureaucracy.

Preservation is relentlessly pragmatic, but imagination refuses to be boxed in. Preservation asks, "Is it realistic, practical, or viable?" Imagination simply replies, "If I can imagine it, it is doable." Preservation says, "We can't go in there; there are giants in the land," but imagination says, "God is with us, we can do it!" (Num. 13.26-33). Preservation requires the rich, powerful, and elite, but imagination can work in *anyone*.

Preservation asks, "How many times should I forgive?" Imagination responds, "I don't know, 70x7?" Imagination plants a tree for shade, while preservation wants to cut it down for firewood. Pharisees wanted rules to follow, but Jesus interpreted the Law in a way that gave freedom and cultivated imagination.

Preservation is not about creating but maintaining. It inspires no one and leads to tiredness, boredom, and lethargy. Prolonged exposure to preservation is dangerous because it atrophies your imagination, turning you into a victim of circumstances. You can become blind to your own shallowness.

Preservation gravitates toward permanent solutions that require no imagination. In the Kingdom the only certainty you have is that there will be uncertainty. The *Mission Impossible* team asked Ethan, "What is the plan?" He replied, "The plan is that the plan is going to change." Since there is no permanent solution, imagination has to resist preservation.

You must crush preservation if you want to cultivate imagination.

Imagination Attracts Critics

As you resist preservation, do not be surprised when you attract critics. Preservation is intolerant and hostile to imagination, because it threatens what they are trying to preserve: their status quo, their life's work, their source of notoriety. Your imagination calls into question the pretense of their agenda. Imagination, hope, and wonder are threatening for people who want to be left alone in the quiet comfort of their situation. People may say they want to be freed by your imaginative ideas but they probably prefer to remain complacently in their present situation.

When false gods are threatened and ridiculed, they fight back. To cultivate imagination is to *launch a revolution*. Preservation attempts to create the pretense that their little world is sufficient and so it is severely resistant to self-criticism. They falsely assume they hold the gold-standard that others want to imitate. They are self-deceived, thinking their influence will live on forever. So they are afraid to hear the truth: they cannot hold on to their share of the pie forever. Preservation is a fading empire that cannot handle the truth about its slow demise.

So people will attempt to drag you down, discourage you, or get you to stop cultivating your imagination. Every imaginative-Nehemiah has his preservationist-Sanballat, someone who does nothing but distract you from your vision (Neh. 4.1-9). They will tell you how raggedy your stuff is; how unprofessional, unsophisticated, or backward. They do so not to provide innovative ideas, but to preserve their share of the pie.

Over the years, several experts from the academic world have told us that The Urban Ministry Institute's sixteen-module *Capstone Curriculum* is sub-standard. They have said that they could make it better by adding their own curriculum to what we have already produced. We call this the "seventeenth module syndrome." Those who represent this syndrome pay no attention to the fact that *Capstone* has effectively trained thousands more leaders than they themselves have trained. So we choose to ignore the critics who hold to preservation, and partner with those who demonstrate imagination.

Imagination Attracts Dependence

When you cultivate imagination, watch out for unhealthy dependence. Because you are an imaginative, fruitful person, others will ask you to carry their load. They will ask you to do things they should do for themselves. Genuine empowerment will not come through pity. You must believe in people enough to let them struggle. You can help, but you can't resolve everything for everyone.

Many ministries and individuals ask us to make exceptions to our protocols because of their "unique situation." We politely refuse because when we do work for people who can do it themselves, we are not empowering, but enabling. This is why our motto at TUMI is borrowed from Home Depot, "You can do it, we can help."

You have to be willing to be misunderstood if you are going to empower others. You must have confidence in your own calling, the resourcing of the Holy Spirit, and the ability of others to cultivate their own imaginations. Beware of unhealthy dependence.

Imagination Is Formed by Anguish

Imagination is not all sweetness and light. In fact, imagination is formed out of a deep longing for things to be different, a discontentment with the status quo. If you ask, "Why can't I shake this persistent grief?" it shows that your imagination is still alive; you haven't fallen victim to the numbness of preservation. Your anguish will drive you to liberate what has become enslaved, to contribute to the collapse of preservation's status quo.

Think about the Israelite nation crying out against Egyptian oppression. Imagination was cultivated once the people had suffered enough to consider leaving the security of Egypt, envisioning a new future as a new people (Exod. 3.9). Imagination envisions a fresh situation, a hopeful set of circumstances. Your work of the Kingdom is to have eyes to see what is bound, seeing into the despair of people, and imagining a different situation.

On the way to my office in South Los Angeles, as I come up from the subway at the corner of Wilshire and Vermont, sometimes I stop for coffee. This is one of the busiest and most diverse intersections in the world. Several ethnic groups walk through the massive courtyard, changing buses, going to school, or rushing to work. I see people of all ages, socioeconomic levels, and occupations. They are lawyers, nurses, students, homeless people, and construction workers. I think about their thoughts and dreams, their hopes and fears. I try to see them as God sees them, people waiting to be liberated into participation in his Kingdom.

Imagination looks beneath the surface of pain and despair and sees a new situation of beauty and hope. Imagination sees what is created in the image of God, waiting to be set free by the Spirit, making people to be who they were meant to be. Imagination is not wiping the slate clean but building on the good that is already there. You need imagination to do that kind of work – to see the good and liberate it.

But that kind of imagination involves anguish and pain. You are in good company because the prophets and apostles before you lived lives of anguished imagination. They knew what it was to invite critics, attract unhealthy dependence, and craft a message out of their anguish. But there is yet another challenge to cultivating your imagination: It takes time, effort, and failure.

Time

A good return on investment takes a long time to produce. Matthew 25.19 says, "Now after a *long time* the master of those servants came and settled accounts with them." The effective stewards, those who doubled the venture capital given to them, took a long time to achieve that return. They did not pursue "get rich quick" schemes.

Imagination waits in expectation that God will give wisdom, but maybe not on your timetable: "They that wait upon the Lord will renew their strength (Isa. 40.31)." This is not a despairing waiting, but an expectant waiting, a peaceful waiting. Imagination is at work while you wait. This is the waiting that the apostles had when Jesus told them to wait for the coming of the Spirit. *Imagination takes time.*

Effort

Imagination also takes effort. It demands discipline, ambition, and courage. God is pleased when you try and fail but displeased when you play it safe, burying his treasure in the ground. The lazy steward was right to say: "I knew you are a hard man, harvesting where you have not sown and gathering where you have not scattered seed (Matt. 25.24)." God wants you to be diligent, using your imagination so he can receive a return on his investment. He wants a harvest as a result of *you* sowing the seeds. He expects you to be clever and work hard to get the job done. *Imagination takes effort.*

Failure

Imagination also involves failure. Many ideas you attempt will not work, some at a laughable level. But God can redeem everything. Innovators value failure because they learn from it. A plant that goes to seed can be the source of a plentiful harvest in the future, so you should cast seed and see what comes up. What seems like a spark of genius might fall flat. Then, to your surprise, a different approach works. Some of my best ideas have come upon second and third attempts. *Imagination takes failure.*

Bringing It All Together

When you aspire to yield an ROI for God, cultivating imagination is more about bravado than technique, more about courage than information, and more about confidence than procedure. It is not just studying the Bible, it is applying biblical truth in creative situations, producing fruit that glorifies his name.

You are fearfully and wonderfully made in the image of God. You are the light of the world (Matt. 5.14). You are his workmanship, created in Christ Jesus to do good works which God prepared beforehand that you should walk in them (Eph. 2.10). With unveiled face, beholding the glory of the Lord, you are being transformed into the same image from one degree of glory to another. For this comes from the Lord who is the Spirit (1 Cor. 3.18).

As you cooperate with the Spirit's forging work, you become his nozzle to deliver living water. When you care for hurting, confused people, devastated by the lies of the evil one, and point them to the life-giving truth of his Word, you produce a return on his investment. *When you cultivate imagination, God can make you into a fruit-making machine!*

But this doesn't stop with you. You can also help others yield their own ROI for God. They learn to demolish strongholds in their own lives, detain thoughts as captives, and defend against disobedience that returns. As they grow in meditation, worship, and praise, they are forged into a nozzle that delivers living water for their network of family and friends.

Conclusion to Part III: You Participate

The devil is eager to pillage by bombarding you with confusing thoughts and feelings. But due to the Father's philanthropy, Jesus's potential, and the Spirit's power, you have weapons to forge your identity to be like Christ. You participate by interrogating thoughts, recognizing lies, and countering with truth (3-D forging). To the extent that you embrace obscurity and cultivate your imagination, you will yield a return on God's investment.

The question before you is clear: Will you *find your identity* (like the world does), or will you allow God to *forge your identity*?

Choose to *Think Again*, in agreement with Don Francisco:[77]

> *Praise the Lord, hallelu, I don't care what the devil's gonna do*
> *The word and faith is my sword and shield,*
> *Jesus is Lord of the way I feel!*

THINK AGAIN

Epilogue

The main idea in this book is simple to understand: believe what is true and extinguish what is false. It's not highly philosophical. It's not mustering up will power, trying harder not to sin. It's believing truth, allowing the Spirit to forge you into a different person at a cellular level.

So you don't have to invest in complicated analysis, discovering the source of the lies. You don't need years of expensive archaeological work, digging into your past. You don't need hours of searching for the source of your polluted stream. Instead, recognize the polluted water and replace it with fresh, living water. Destroy toxic branches in your brain by replacing them with life-giving branches. As you allow the Spirit to forge your identity, he demolishes strongholds and forms new DNA that reflects the life of Jesus.

Although it is simple to comprehend, it is neither quick nor easy. It takes time to be forged because strongholds were built over many years. Renewing your mind requires perseverance. Forging is not easy because no discipline is pleasant at the time, but painful. But if you are willing to be trained through the hardship, God promises to produce a return on investment (Heb. 12.11).

A Second Read

This book was designed to encourage you, to make you more productive for his Kingdom. I challenge you to read it and re-read it because every believer is in constant need of on-going transformation. You will never outgrow the need for 3-D forging. You will never be so wise that you don't have to stop and *Think Again*.

The first time through, you should read it for yourself. But a second reading can be useful in helping others, discipling them to yield an ROI for the Kingdom. Use this book for soul care, discipleship, and leadership development.

While the principles and practices are designed for the adult believer, they can also be helpful in raising children to live a wise and fruitful life. Whether children decide to follow the Lord as adults or not, they will be stronger people if they learn from a young age to recognize lies and embrace truth. If you are a parent, grandparent, aunt, or Sunday school teacher having influence in a child's life, re-read this book with them in mind.

Don't Deny Your Pain

Think Again is not an endorsement of triumphalism or positive confession. The beauty of the Spirit's forging is that you don't have to deny your pain. You don't need to live in fear that you somehow bring trouble upon yourself by admitting your feelings.

On the contrary, you can agree with Jesus by saying, "In this world you will have tribulation" (John 16.33). Like Paul, you can admit that you experience distress, persecution, famine, nakedness, danger, or sword (Rom. 8.35). You can find comfort from James, that despite facing trials of many kinds, you can count it all joy (James 1.2-4). Because you are called not only to believe in him, but to suffer for him, you can freely acknowledge your heartaches (Phil. 1.29). It doesn't do you any good to ignore the misery you feel.

But despite all your vexations, remember that nothing begins to compare to the glory that awaits you: "*For this light momentary affliction is preparing for us an eternal weight of glory beyond all comparison, as we look not to the things that are seen but to the things that are unseen. For the things that are seen are transient, but the things that are unseen are eternal*" (2 Cor. 4.17-18). Praise God!!

I pray you will *Think Again*, participating with Jesus to change the world!

THINK AGAIN

Appendices

Appendix 1

Common Lies That Create Strongholds

The following are *lies* that masquerade as truth, from *Telling Yourself the Truth.*[78]

1. The way to be liked by others is to be what others want me to be and to do what is most pleasing to them.
2. It is wrong and un-Christian to think of my own needs, or to consider my own needs important.
3. I should forget my own wants to please friends and family when they want me to.
4. Pleasing others is an insurance policy which guarantees that people will be nice to me in return. When I am in great need they will forget their own needs to help me.
5. When others are displeased with me, I cannot enjoy one moment's peace or happiness.
6. Approval from everyone else is essential to my feeling of well-being and peace of mind.
7. God doesn't want me to be happy unless everyone else is approving of me.
8. Being what other people want me to be is the only way to be liked.
9. Pleasing others and doing what they expect of me is the only way to find friends.
10. If I don't give, give, give, I'm not a good Christian.
11. I must be appreciated for all I give.

12. My self-worth depends of the opinions of other people.
13. If I don't do what other people want and expect me to do, they won't like me.
14. If I don't do what other people want me to do, I don't deserve their approval or friendship.
15. Other people have the right to ask anything they want of me in order that I won't offend anyone.
16. If others do not tell me I am a good person, then I must not be.
17. If someone does not like me, there is something wrong with me.
18. If someone is angry with me, it must be my fault.
19. It's my duty to make everybody happy and comfortable.
20. It's my duty to work my fingers to the bone for my family. If I don't, they might reject me.
21. In spite of how hard I work to earn approval, some people still don't like me and reject me; therefore I am terrible.
22. It's awful to be angry. I am angry; therefore I am awful.
23. It's terrible to be a thing other people use. I am a thing other people use; therefore I am terrible.
24. I can't conquer my bad feelings. Therefore, I am terrible.
25. I'm the way I am because I was born that way.
26. If I had a better education, I'd be better liked.
27. If I were like so-and-so I'd be a happier person.
28. If I were better looking, I'd be a happier person.

29. It's not what you know; it's who you know. That's why I'm not more successful.
30. If only I lived in a better neighborhood. Then I'd be happy.
31. This house depresses me.
32. I know I should change but I just can't.
33. The reason I drink is because of the pressures that I face every day.
34. The reason I curse is because everyone at the office curses.
35. The reason I steal is because my boss is too cheap to give me the raise I deserve.

Appendix 2

Using the Armor of God

> Finally, be strong in the Lord and in the strength of his might. [11] Put on the whole armor of God, that you may be able to stand against the schemes of the devil. [12] For we do not wrestle against flesh and blood, but against the rulers, against the authorities, against the cosmic powers over this present darkness, against the spiritual forces of evil in the heavenly places. [13] Therefore take up the whole armor of God, that you may be able to withstand in the evil day, and having done all, to stand firm. [14] Stand therefore, having fastened on the belt of truth, and having put on the breastplate of righteousness, [15] and, as shoes for your feet, having put on the readiness given by the gospel of peace. [16] In all circumstances take up the shield of faith, with which you can extinguish all the flaming darts of the evil one; [17] and take the helmet of salvation, and the sword of the Spirit, which is the word of God, [18] praying at all times in the Spirit, with all prayer and supplication. To that end keep alert with all perseverance, making supplication for all the saints, [19] and also for me, that words may be given to me in opening my mouth boldly to proclaim the mystery of the gospel, [20] for which I am an ambassador in chains, that I may declare it boldly, as I ought to speak.
>
> ~ Ephesians 6.10-20

What a delicious passage! It serves as a way to bring together the entire book of Ephesians, packaging all the previous points into a concise, cosmic message. It forms an actionable whole. The word "finally" (v.10) is not the last point in a series; it's not like saying "buy milk, eggs, butter, and *finally* cake mix." It is more like saying, "pick up milk, eggs, butter, cake mix, and *finally* make a cake." In that sense, this passage is a summary of the whole book of Ephesians.

We

In verse 12, Paul says that we wrestle (we don't do this alone). While this passage is often taught as a personal struggle, the whole book of Ephesians underscores that the Christian life is to be lived together with other believers. Walter Wink noted, "The metaphor of the church is like the Roman wedge, the most efficient and terrifying military formation known to that time and for some thousand years later. In fact, the instruction in this whole section is plural."[79]

When we recognize the full weight of danger we face against the evil one, we will instinctively draw near to our comrades, even those with whom we may not otherwise be friends. Those who cause division show they don't recognize the terrible threat that is around them. They put themselves in harms way by going it alone.

Wrestle

Next, Paul reminds us this is a *wrestling* match. As a child, I went to a summer sports camp that introduced me to several sports including wrestling. I quickly learned to hate wrestling. It was so sweaty, so invasive of another person's body. Wrestling involves all-out energy, struggling against another person as you look at him in the face. As much as I despised it, wrestling is a good metaphor for the Christian life, because we engage an opponent in a visceral way. This battle is not like the image of remotely-located generals, lobbing missiles at far-away armies. This is hand-to-hand combat; messy, full of smoke, explosions, confusion, pain, and screaming.

True Enemies

Paul also dismisses any notion that people are our enemies. We don't wrestle with flesh and blood. The true source of attacks against includes rulers, authorities, cosmic powers, spiritual forces of evil. The image is of unseen, constant schemes directed at us from every direction. Every problem has a cosmic origin, not a human one.

Schemes

We are to withstand these schemes, having done all to stand firm. We must not be dispossessed, conned by Satan's schemes. Scripture points to several references about the adversary's tactics: deceit, doubt, intimidation, alternative solutions, division, harassment, confusion, surprise.

Eve was tempted to distrust God through *deceit and doubt*. "God is withholding good from you, so take matters in your own hands." The tragic result was that humanity was dispossessed of paradise.

Job was tempted to "curse God to His face" through *intimidation*. The enemy sought to frighten Job through the death of loved ones, financial losses, and health problems – all made worse by unhelpful friends.

Jesus was tempted by schemes to disrupt God's plan through *alternative solutions*. The enemy offered Jesus a shortcut to achieve the Father's goals. First, Jesus was offered immediate gratification (turning stone to bread). But Jesus resisted, showing his trust in the Father for his needs. Next, he was offered influence and authority over all the kingdoms of the world. But Jesus refused the shortcut to the Father's path to greatness (which would be through the humiliation of the cross). Finally, Jesus was offered notoriety and applause (by jumping off temple in spectacular style). But he trusted God for his fame, which we know is coming when "every knee will bow and tongue confess Jesus as Lord" (Phil. 2.9-11). Jesus will receive his rightful accolades, but only because he refused Satan's alternative solutions.

The apostles explained how the evil one uses *division, harassment, confusion, and surprise.*

- *Division*: Paul warns believers in Ephesians 4.27 to avoid giving the devil a foothold. In-fighting and disunity are a dead giveaway that the enemy is affecting a situation.
- *Harassment*: In Acts 16, a fortune-telling evil spirit pesters Paul for many days.
- *Confusion*: In 2 Corinthians 11.13-14, Satan is said to masquerade as angel of light.
- *Surprise*: In Peter 4.12, Peter says we "do not be surprised at the fiery trial when it comes upon you to test you, as though something strange were happening to you."

Deceit, doubt, intimidation, alternative solutions, division, harassment, confusion, and surprise are some of the devil's schemes. But God doesn't leave us defenseless. We have equipment and weapons to fight the adversary's schemes of dispossession. We have armor to fight off his attacks.

Actualize the Weapons

We have power to defend our treasure, but we have to competently use the weapons he provides. We have to use our mind, will, and emotions to make the equipment effective:

Because Of:	We Need:
Deceit	A belt of **truth** (countering lies and half-truths)
Division and alternative solutions	A breastplate of **righteousness** (building right relationships with God and others)
Surprise and intimidation	Shoes of **readiness** (maintaining vigilance)
Flaming darts of confusion	A shield of **faith** (having confidence in the middle of trials)
Doubt about our eternal security	A helmet of **salvation** (believing in the certainty of our future)
Harassment	A sword of the **Spirit guided by prayer** (handling chaotic and dynamic situations with wisdom)

Truth

The belt serves to integrate all the armor together. God is the God of all truth, not just truth from the Bible. Truth helps us recognize lies, and allows us to live a life of integrity, being aligned with the truth in our every aspect of life.

Righteousness

We need righteousness to protect us. Righteousness is not just personal ethics, but *right relationships* within a community. The breastplate serves as a shorthand for the many "one-another" commands: humility, gentleness, patience, love, forgiveness, kindness, joy, thanksgiving, mutual submission. The breastplate keeps us from ruining our human relationships and also breaking relationship with God. When tempted by alternative solutions,

Jesus trusted God for provision. In the same way the breastplate protects us from ruining our relationship with God through sin.

Readiness

We need readiness to protect us from being caught off guard. We are surprised by health problems, unexpected death, or financial challenges. The Roman shoes of readiness had spikes to grip the ground, like modern baseball batters who dig their cleats in for traction.

In the Already/Not-Yet Kingdom, it is inevitable that we will experience suffering. This helps us deal with the element of surprise. Paul said not to be discouraged by his suffering because it was their glory (Eph. 3.13). He said to look carefully how you walk because the days are evil (Eph. 5.15). Jesus said, "In this world you will have tribulation, but be of good cheer for I have overcome the world" (John 16.33).

The readiness (given by the gospel of peace) is more than just personal salvation by grace. It has a much more transcendent view, where God revealed "his will, according to his purpose, which he set forth in Christ as a plan for the fullness of time, to unite all things in him, things in heaven and things on earth" (Eph. 1.10). The gospel is Good News that *all of creation* will be made brand new (Rev. 21.5). The readiness given by the gospel is confidence that "he put all things under his feet and gave him as head over all things" (Eph. 1.22).

We wear shoes of readiness to stand our ground, to stand firm and to remain calm and peaceful in the midst of a cosmic battle.

Faith

The shield of faith protects us from getting confused about God's goodness. We can have confidence in what we hope for, certainty of what we don't see (Heb. 11.1). We walk by faith not by sight (2 Cor. 5.7). We believe the unseen truth when all the visible evidence is just the opposite.

The devil's schemes are designed to cause distrust and lead to dispossession. They play on our fears, when we should trust God for our needs. Every temptation is a scheme to distrust God, to drop our shield of faith. He urges us to trust our feelings and throw away our confidence in God. Eve gave in and lost faith, but Jesus stood firm and trusted the Father by faith.

The flaming darts mentioned in this passage were arrows covered in pitch, and if they connected and lodged in a soldier, the soldier would suffer burns. The Roman shield was made of materials that would extinguish the flames on impact. It was not an individual shield, but a large interlocking network of shields that connected fellow soldiers, protecting everyone from all angles so no one had any cracks in their armor. So if a soldier isolated himself and pulled away, he would lose the protection of the unit.

Paul wanted to make sure we don't fight this fight alone, but together. When we separate from the body, we put too much pressure on ourselves, which makes us vulnerable to flaming arrows of distraction. The truth is we are not alone. God is with us and the body is there to link our shields together for protection.

Salvation

When soldiers are hit in the head without a helmet, they become disoriented. In the same way, if we doubt salvation, we become dazed, and vulnerable to other kinds of attacks. We need assurance of salvation to keep our wits about us. So the enemy will tell us that we are not saved. If we *believe* that we are not saved, we will start *acting* like we are not saved. Having confidence in our eternal security is fundamental to spiritual warfare.

The Spirit and Prayer

We need the Holy Spirit to help us use the Word, and prayer helps us engage the various trials and situations that emerge. The Bible (the sword of the Spirit) should be used with skill and guidance in conjunction with prayer. We are constantly thrown into situations that need all kinds of wisdom. Dr. Don Davis has referred to prayer as the "walkie-talkie of faith." Through prayer, we ask for the necessary firepower we need in precarious situations.

The truth of God's Word needs to be applied with dexterity and wisdom. We apply offensive tactics, resisting the devil so he will flee (James 4.7; 1 Pet. 5.9). We also keep alert with perseverance. We pray for one another because if I am not in a chaotic moment, it is guaranteed that others are. The Spirit is constantly at work, giving us power, and making his Word known to us. As the Author of the Bible, he guides us to handle the Word while we pray all manner of prayers for ourselves and others.

To Advance the Gospel

In all this use of armor, we long to advance the gospel (Eph. 6.19-20). Paul asks for prayer, summarizing all the previously mentioned themes of Ephesians:

- We have riches beyond description
- We have an adversary trying to dispossess us
- We have power and equipment to resist our dispossession

Christ Is Our Armor

The armor is given to us, and we must exercise our mind, will, and emotions to engage in spiritual warfare. But in another sense, the armor is a picture of God's provision in Christ. In several places we are told to "put on Christ" (Rom. 13.4; Col. 3.12;

Eph. 4.24). As we become integrated and forged into Christ, we take on all his attributes.

The elements of the armor can all be related to Christ himself. We engage the enemy with power that is not our own, because we are united as a body to the Head.

- He is our belt of truth (the Way, the Truth, and the Life, John 14.6).
- He is our breastplate of righteousness (1 Cor. 1.30).
- He is our shoes of readiness (who will soon crush Satan under our feet, Rom. 16.20).
- He is our shield of faith (the Author and Perfecter of our Faith, Heb. 12.2).
- He is our salvation (the helmet of salvation, Isa. 59).
- He is our sword (the Word of God, John 1.1).

Take up the whole armor of God, that you may be able to withstand in the evil day, and having done all, to stand firm!

Appendix 3

Who Am I?

The following are affirmations of identity from *Victory over the Darkness*:[80]

1. I am Christ's friend (John 15.15).
2. I am chosen and appointed by Christ to bear his fruit (John 15.16).
3. I am a slave of righteousness (Rom. 6.18).
4. I am enslaved to God (Rom. 6.22).
5. I am a son of God; God is spiritually my Father (Rom. 8.14-15; Gal. 3.26; 4.6).
6. I am a joint heir with Christ, sharing His inheritance with him (Rom. 8.17).
7. I am a temple, a dwelling place of God. His Spirit and his life dwell in me (1 Cor. 3.16; 6.19).
8. I am united to the Lord and am one in spirit with him (1 Cor. 6.17).
9. I am a member of Christ's body (1 Cor. 12.27; Eph. 5.30).
10. I am a new creation (2 Cor. 5.17).
11. I am reconciled to God and am a minister of reconciliation (2 Cor. 5.18-19).
12. I am a son of God and one in Christ (Gal. 3.26-28).
13. I am an heir of God since I am a son of God (Gal. 6.4,7).

14. I am a saint (1 Cor. 1.2; Eph. 1.1; Phil. 1.1; Col. 1.2).
15. I am God's workmanship, his handiwork, born anew in Christ to do his work (Eph. 2.10).
16. I am a fellow citizen with the rest of God's family (Eph. 2.19).
17. I am a prisoner of Christ (Eph. 3.1; 4.1).
18. I am righteous and holy (Eph. 4.24).
19. I am a citizen of heaven, seated in heaven right now (Eph. 2.5; Phil. 3.20).
20. I am hidden with Christ in God (Col. 3.3).
21. I am an expression of the life of Christ because he is my life (Col. 3.4).
22. I am chosen of God, holy and dearly loved (Col. 3.12; Thess. 1.4).
23. I am a son of light and not of darkness (1 Thess. 5.5).
24. I am a holy partaker of a heavenly calling (Heb. 3.1).
25. I am a partaker of Christ; I share in his life (Heb. 3.14).
26. I am one of God's living stones, being built up in Christ as a spiritual house (1 Pet. 2.5).
27. I am a member of a chosen race, a royal priesthood, a holy nation, a people for God's own possession (1 Pet. 2.2,10).
28. I am an alien and stranger to this world in which I temporarily live (1 Pet. 2.11).
29. I am an enemy of the devil (1 Pet. 5.8).

30. I am a child of God and I will resemble Christ when he returns (1 John 3.1-2).

31. I am born of God so the evil one, the devil, cannot touch me (1 John 5.18).

32. I am not the great "I am" (Exod. 3.14; John 8.24, 25, 58), but by the grace of God, I am what I am (1 Cor. 15.10).

Appendix 4

Thoughts on Spiritual Disciplines

I. Rev. Dr. Don L. Davis offers this tour de force for understanding and practicing spiritual disciplines, exploring the following ideas:[81]

A. The Disciplined Life

B. The Celebrations of a Disciplined Life

C. Cultivating Our Communion: The Inward Disciplines (The Word, Prayer, Fasting, Study)

D. Cultivating Our Character: The Outward Disciplines (Simplicity, Solitude, Submission, Service)

E. Cultivating Our Community: The Corporate Disciplines (Confession, Worship, Guidance, Celebration)

F. Fleshing Out a Compelling Testimony: Disciplining our Disciplines

II. J.P. Moreland provides excellent insight about spiritual disciplines.[82]

A. He describes spiritual disciplines and their effect on our sanctification using a comparison to golf: "When people play golf, they have a 'golf character,' that is, the sum of a person's bad golf habits. A golf game may be weakened by bad habits in the wrists, shoulders, or somewhere else. People may have good habits in their legs but bad habits (golf flesh) in their shoulders. How does one develop a good golf character? Not simply by daily golf readings coupled with regular exposure to motivational golf music! No, golfers present their members to a golf instructor at a driving range as instruments of 'golf righteousness.' By presenting their members, they gradually get rid of bad golf habits and replace them with good ones, repeatedly engaging specific body parts in regular activities done over and over again, with the instructor in charge."

B. Moreland organizes disciplines in two categories:

1. Disciplines of Abstinence: Solitude, Silence, Fasting, Frugality, Chastity, Secrecy, Sacrifice

2. Disciplines of Engagement: Study, Worship, Celebration, Service, Prayer, Fellowship, Confession, Submission

III. Dallas Willard offered these helpful quotes about disciplines.[83]

A. "A discipline is any activity within our power that we engage in to enable us to do what we cannot do by direct effort."

B. "They are disciplines designed to help us be active and effective in the spiritual realm of our own heart, now spiritually alive by grace, in relation to God and his Kingdom. They are designed to help us withdraw from total dependence on the merely human or natural (and in that precise sense to mortify the 'flesh,' kill it off, let it die) and to depend also on the ultimate reality, which is God and his Kingdom. Thus, for example, I fast from food to know that there is another food that sustains me. I memorize and meditate on scripture that the order of

God's Kingdom would become the order and power of my mind and my life."

C. "The disciplines do not confirm their value to those who only talk about them or study them 'academically' or hear others talk about them. One has to enter them with Jesus as teacher to find the incredible power they have to change one's world and character. They are self-confirming when entered in faith and humility. And you don't really need much of faith and humility if you will just stay with them. They will do the rest because they open us to the Kingdom. This is an extension of Jesus's emphasis on doing as a way of knowing the Kingdom. We will be able to do what he says to do as we are inwardly transformed by following him into his life practices of solitude, service, study, and so forth. This is an essential part of what Paul calls 'offering our bodies as living sacrifices' (Rom. 12.2). It will result in the mark of the disciplined person, who is able to do what needs to be done when and as it needs to be done."

D. "In particular, I had learned that intensity is crucial for any progress in spiritual perception and understanding. To dribble a few verses or chapters of Scripture on oneself through the week, in church or out, will not reorder one's mind and spirit – just as one drop of water every five minutes will not get you a shower, no matter how long you keep it up. You need a lot of water at once and for a sufficiently long time. Similarly for the written Word."

E. "In particular I did not understand the intensity with which they must be done, nor that the appropriate intensity required that they be engaged in for lengthy periods of undistracted time on a single occasion. Moreover, one's life as a whole had to be arranged in such a way that this would be possible. One must not be agitated, hurried, or exhausted when the time of prayer and study came. Hence one cannot tack an effective, life-transforming practice of prayer and study onto 'life as usual.' Life as usual must go. It will be replaced by something far better."

F. "What is clear and, for our purposes, essential is that a small number of them are absolutely central to spiritual growth. They must form a part of the foundation of our whole-life plan for growth as apprentices of Jesus. These are, on the side of abstinence, solitude and silence and, on the side of positive engagement, study and worship."

G. "You will know this finding of soul and God is happening by an increased sense of who you are and a lessening of the feeling that you have to do this, that, and the other thing that befalls your lot in life. That harassing, hovering feeling of 'have to' largely comes from the vacuum in your soul, where you ought to be at home with your Father in his Kingdom. As the vacuum is rightly filled, you will increasingly know that you do not have to do those things – not even those you want to do."

H. "Liberation from your own desires is one of the greatest gifts of solitude and silence. When this all begins to happen, you will know you are arriving where you ought to be. Old bondages to wrongdoing will begin to drop off as you see them for what they are. And the possibility of really loving people will dawn upon you. Soon you may even come to know what it is like to live by grace rather than just talk about it."

Appendix 5

Practical Steps When You Feel Overwhelmed

1. Pay attention to the basics. "*Live in harmony with the physical design protocols for life, such as regular sleep, drink plenty of water, exercise mind and body regularly, avoid toxins, and eat a balanced diet. When mistakes are made, resolve guilt as soon as possible, forgive those who mistreat you, and don't hold to anger or grudges as such emotions activate the body's inflammatory cascade. Resolve fear, as unremedied fear truly destroys. It is love that heals and restores, but genuine love is only experienced when lies about God are removed*" (Dr. Timothy Jennings).[84]

2. Ask God, what should I do next? Don't solve everything at once. Just take the next step. Once you know the next step, do the next thing well.

3. Shorten the response time between falling and getting up. We all fall and make mistakes, but the difference is how quickly we get up from falling. Does it take a minute, a day, a week, or a year for you to respond to God's leading and get back up on your feet?

4. To find peace and liberty, follow the advice of Thomas á Kempis:[85]

    a. Strive to do another's will rather than your own.

    b. Choose always to have less than more.

    c. Seek lower places in life, putting to death the need to be recognized and important.

    d. Always and in everything desire that the will of God completely fulfilled in you.

Appendix 6

Selected Quotes on Narcissism

I. In his book, *The Culture of Narcissism: American Life in an Age of Diminishing Expectations*,[86] Christopher Lasch makes the point that psychological problems change over time and across different cultures. What was common in the first half of the 20th century was different than the last half of the century. This suggests to me that the work of principalities and powers understand which deceptions are most effective in each culture, place, or time. Demonic efforts to steal, kill, and destroy are adapted to fit a cultural setting in order to keep people bound and under their controlling influence. Since the 1950s in the USA, narcissism appears to have been the strategy of choice for evil spirits to do their pillaging work. If so, it is helpful to know more about narcissism as a cluster of lies that is keeping Americans bound. People in other cultures will experience a different cluster of lies. The following are selected quotes from Lasch's book (which is not written from a Christian perspective).

A. "People have convinced themselves that what matters is psychic self-improvement: getting in touch with their feelings, eating health food, taking lessons in ballet or belly-dancing, immersing themselves in the wisdom of the East, jogging, learning how to 'relate,' overcoming the 'fear of pleasure'" (p. 4).

B. "He complains 'of vague, diffuse dissatisfactions with life' and feels his 'amorphous existence to be futile and purposeless.' He describes 'subtly experienced yet pervasive feelings of emptiness and depression,' 'violent oscillations of self-esteem,' and 'a general inability to get along.' He gains 'a sense of heightened self-esteem only by attaching himself to strong, admired figures whose acceptance he craves and by whom he needs to feel supported.' Although he carries out his daily responsibilities and even achieves distinction, happiness eludes him, and life frequently strikes him as not worth living. Often these patients suffer from hypochondria and complain of a sense of inner emptiness. At the same time they entertain fantasies of omnipotence and a strong belief in their right to exploit others and be gratified" (p. 37).

C. "Although the narcissist can function in the everyday world and often charms other people, his devaluation of others, together with his lack of curiosity about them, impoverishes his personal life and reinforces the 'subjective experience of emptiness'" (p. 39).

D. "He therefore depends on others for constant infusions of approval and admiration. He 'must attach [himself] to someone, living an almost parasitic' existence. At the same time, his fear of emotional dependence, together with his manipulative, exploitive approach to personal relations, makes these relations bland, superficial, and deeply unsatisfying" (p. 40).

E. "In a society that dreads old age and death, aging holds a special terror for those who fear dependence and whose self-esteem requires the admiration usually reserved for youth, beauty, celebrity, or charm. The usual defenses against the ravages of age – identification with ethical or artistic values beyond one's immediate interests, intellectual curiosity, the consoling emotional warmth derived from happy relationships in the past – can do nothing for the narcissist. To be able to enjoy life in a process involving a growing identification with other people's happiness and achievements is tragically beyond the capacity of narcissistic personalities" (p. 41).

F. "He wants to 'be known as a winner, and his deepest fear is to be labeled a loser.' Instead of pitting himself against a material task or a problem demanding solution, he pits himself against others, out of a 'need to be in control.' As a recent textbook for managers puts it, success today means 'not simply getting ahead' but 'getting ahead of others.' He has little capacity for 'personal intimacy and social commitment'" (p. 44).

G. "In the first three centuries of our history, the work ethic constantly changed its meaning. For the Puritans, a godly man worked diligently at his calling not so much in order to accumulate personal wealth as to add to the comfort and convenience of the community. Every Christian had a 'general calling' to serve God and a 'personal calling.' The Puritans recognized that a man might get rich at his calling, but they saw personal aggrandizement as incidental to social labor – the collective transformation of nature and the progress of useful arts and useful knowledge. They instructed men who prospered not to lord it over their neighbors. The true Christian, according to Calvinist conceptions of an honorable and godly existence, bore both good fortune and bad with equanimity, contenting himself with what came to his lot" (p. 53).

H. "Those who win the attention of the public worry incessantly about losing it. . . . He confuses successful completion of the task at hand with the impression he makes or hopes to make on others. . . . Impressions overshadow achievements" (p. 60).

I. "He advances through the corporate ranks not by serving the organization but by convincing his associates that he possesses the attributes of a 'winner'" (p. 61).

J. "Narcissistic patients 'are afraid of not belonging to the company of the great, rich, and powerful, and of belonging instead to the mediocre, by which they mean worthless and despicable rather than average in the ordinary sense of the term.' They worship heroes only to turn against them when their heroes disappoint them" (p. 84).

K. "We seek reassurance of our capacity to captivate or impress others, anxiously searching out blemishes that might detract from the appearance we intend to project. The advertising industry deliberately encourages this preoccupation with appearances. In the twenties, 'the women in ads were constantly observing themselves, ever self-critical. A noticeable proportion of magazine ads directed at women depicted them looking into mirrors. Ads of the 1920s were quite explicit about this narcissistic imperative'" (p. 92).

L. "He extols cooperation and teamwork while harboring deeply antisocial impulses. He praises respect for rules and regulations in the secret belief that they do not apply to himself. Acquisitive in the sense that his cravings have no limits, he does not accumulate goods and provisions against the future, in the manner of the acquisitive individualist of nineteenth-century political economy, but demands immediate gratification and lives in a state of restless, perpetually unsatisfied desire" (p. 172).

M. "What says 'you are not guilty' says also 'you cannot help yourself.' Therapy legitimates deviance as sickness, but it simultaneously pronounces the patient unfit to manage his own life and delivers him into the hands of a specialist. As therapeutic points of view and practice gain general acceptance, more and more people find themselves disqualified, in effect, from the performance of adult responsibilities and become dependent on some form of medical authority" (p. 230).

II. The following are selected quotes from *Overcoming the Dark Side of Leadership*, Gary L. McIntosh and Samuel D. Rima.[87]

A. "For the narcissistic leader, the world revolves on the axis of self, and all other people and issues closely orbit them as they get caught in the strong gravitational pull of the narcissist's self-absorption. Narcissistic leaders 'present various combinations of intense ambitiousness, grandiose fantasies, feelings of inferiority and over dependence on external admiration and acclaim.' At the same time a self-absorbed leader is chronically uncertain of himself and experiences dissatisfaction with his accomplishments, which he tries to overcome by exploiting others in ways that will help elevate his self-image. In addition, narcissistic leaders have an overinflated sense of their importance to the organization and have an exhibitionistic need for constant attention and admiration from others, especially those they lead and any person or group to whom they report. In spite of their drive to achieve greatness, their restless ambition is rarely satisfied in a way that enables them to enjoy their accomplishments. Another characteristic is their 'interpersonal exploitiveness,' in which others are taken advantage in order to indulge [their] own desires or for self-aggrandizement."

B. "Narcissistic leaders also tend to overestimate their own achievements and abilities while stubbornly refusing to recognize the quality and value of the same in others. Any recognition of someone else's accomplishments or abilities is a threat to their own self-importance and risks the loss of the exclusive admiration they crave from their followers. Because narcissistic leaders tend to use others to advance their own goals, they are notorious for being unable to empathize with those they lead. This enables them to pursue their own ends without restraints. Though narcissism seems to be diametrically opposed to the concept of spiritual, servant leadership, it is all too common in the church and among spiritual leadership."

C. "Christian leaders often use those they lead to enhance their own image and improve the way they feel about themselves. Far too many sermons are preached in an effort to gain the approval and admiration of followers, with little or no concern for God's approval. The pastor or speaker who steps down from the platform and is immediately obsessed with whether his sermon was good is dealing with a prime symptom of narcissism."

D. "Numerous churches have been destroyed by leaders who led the church into projects too energetic and costly for the congregation because he needed to feel good about himself. How easy it is for Christian leaders to use their organizations as nothing more than platforms from which they launch themselves on their chosen career path with little or no regard for the long-term health of the organization they were entrusted to lead."

E. "When a pastor or Christian executive says to himself, 'This church (or organization) would suffer if I ever left,' it is a sign of narcissism. When the leader is constantly beginning new ministries, even when existing, essential ministries are not adequately staffed or effective, this is a sign of narcissism. Rather than ensuring that existing ministries are efficiently functioning, the narcissistic leader needs the kudos that come from new and unique ministries. However, once the 'high' of a new ministry launch is gone, the narcissistic leader provides little long-term oversight or maintenance."

F. "Because ministry provides the ready justification that grandiose visions and risky ventures are necessary to accomplish God's kingdom work, the church and Christian organizations provide fertile soil for budding narcissists. Tragically, because many followers of the narcissistic leader think all this activity is being done for God, they feel uncomfortable challenging their leader."

THINK AGAIN

Endnotes

1. Moreland, J. P. *The God Question*. Eugene, OR: Harvest House Publisher, 2009, p. 32.
2. Iyengar, Sheena. *The Art of Choosing*. New York, NY: Grand Central Publishing, 2010, p. 82-83.
3. Ibid., p. 104.
4. For selected quotes about Narcissism, see Appendix 6.
5. Moreland, J. P. *The God Question*, p. 14.
6. Anderson, Neil. *Victory over the Darkness*. Ventura, CA: Regal Books, 1990, p. 27.
7. Murphy, Edward. *The Handbook of Spiritual Warfare*. Nashville, TN: Thomas Nelson Publishers, Inc., 1992, 1996, 2003, p. 71.
8. Tozer, A. W. *The Divine Conquest*. Living Books Publisher, 1995, p. 40.
9. Jones, E. Stanley. *The Way to Power and Poise*. Nashville, TN: Abingdon-Cokesbury 1949, p. vii.
10. Backus, William and Marie Chapian. *Telling Yourself the Truth*. Minneapolis, MN: Bethany House Publishers, 1980, 1981, 2000, p. 29.
11. Anderson, Neil. *Victory over the Darkness*, p. 49.
12. Willard, Dallas. *The Divine Conspiracy*. New York, NY: HarperCollins Publishers, 1998, p. 383.

13. Lewis, C. S. *Mere Christianity*. Macmillan Publishers, 1952, p. 46.

14. Jennings, Timothy. *The God-Shaped Brain: How Changing Your View of God Transforms Your Life*. Downers Grove, IL: Inter Varsity Press, 2013, p. 54.

15. Anderson, Neil T. *Victory over the Darkness*, p. 159.

16. https://afsp.org/about-suicide/suicide-statistics/

17. Moreland, J. P. *The God Question*, p. 212.

18. Backus, William and Marie Chapian. *Telling Yourself the Truth*, p. 86-87.

19. Leaf, Caroline. *Switch On Your Brain*. Grand Rapids, MI: Baker Books Publisher, 2013, p. 63.

20. Iyengar, Sheena. *The Art of Choosing*, p. 28.

21. Fee, Gordon. *Paul, The Spirit, and the People of God*. Grand Rapids, MI: Baker Academic,1996, p. 127.

22. Lewis, C. S. *Mere Christianity*. Macmillan Publishers, 1952, p. 168.

23. Chole, Alicia. *Anonymous: Jesus' hidden years . . . and yours*. Nashville, TN: Thomas Nelson, 2006, Kindle location 1098.

24. Willard, Dallas. *The Divine Conspiracy*, p. 344.

25. Modis, Theodore. *Conquering Uncertainty*. McGraw-Hill, 1998.

26. Willard, Dallas. *The Divine Conspiracy*, p. 82.

27. https://www.goodreads.com/quotes/8202-the-mass-of-men-lead-lives-of-quiet-desperation-what

28. Batterson, Mark. *Primal: A Quest for the Lost Soul of Christianity*. Multnomah Books, 2009, p. 112.

29. For an excellent book on the Already/Not-yet Kingdom, see *The Gospel of the Kingdom* by George Ladd, 1959.

30. Willard, Dallas. *The Divine Conspiracy*, p. 329.

31. Davis, Don. *Capstone Curriculum, Module #6, God the Father*. Wichita, KS: The Urban Ministry Institute, 2005, p. 5-6.

32. Willard, Dallas. *The Divine Conspiracy*, p. 338.

33. Leaf, Caroline. *Switch On Your Brain*, p. 14.

34. Ibid., p. 19-20.

35. Ibid., p. 35.

36. Ibid., p. 64.

37. Willard, Dallas. *The Divine Conspiracy*, p. 62.

38. Gregory of Nyssa, *Devotional Classics*, edited by Richard Foster and James Bryan Smith. New York, NY: HarperCollins Publishers, 1990, p. 125.

39. Dallas Willard, *The Divine Conspiracy*, p. 379.

40. https://www.goodreads.com/quotes/582528-one-must-face-the-fact-that-all-the-talk-about

41. An excellent source for helping others in their pain is *Connecting* by Larry Crabb. 1997.

42. Chole, Alicia. *Anonymous: Jesus' hidden years . . . and yours*, Kindle location 488.

43. Chan, Simon. *Liturgical Theology*. Downers Grove, IL: InterVarsity Press, 2006, p. 33. Simon Chan, p. 36.

44. Ibid.

45. Ibid., p. 33-37.

46. Fee, Gordon. *Paul, The Spirit, and the People of God*, p. 7.

47. Ibid., p. xv.

48. Chan, Simon. *Liturgical Theology*, p. 60.

49. Fee, Gordon. *Paul, The Spirit, and the People of God*, p. 103.

50. Batterson, Mark. *Wild Goose Chase*. Colorado Springs, CO: Multnomah Books, 2008, p. 6.

51. Anderson, Neil. *Victory over the Darkness*, p. 97.

52. http://webcache.googleusercontent.com/search?q=cache:-snfnWqSNIAJ:www.mentalhealthamerica.net/recognizing-warning-signs+&cd=16&hl=en&ct=clnk&gl=us&client=firefox-b

53. Crabb, Larry. *Connecting*. Nashville, TN: Word Publishing, 1997, p. 91.

54. Moreland, J. P. *The God Question*, p. 203-204.

55. Leaf, Caroline. *Switch On Your Brain*, p. 47.

56. Crabb, Larry. *Connecting*, p. 91.

57. Backus, William and Marie Chapian. *Telling Yourself the Truth*, p. 65.

58. Fee, Gordon. *Paul, The Spirit, and the People of God*, p. 138.

59. Chole, Alicia. *Anonymous: Jesus' hidden years . . . and yours*, Kindle Location 485.

60. For example, see https://www.joystartshere.com/site/doc/JoyfulJourneyQuestions.pdf and lifemodelworks.org.

61. Leaf, Caroline. *Switch On Your Brain*, part 2, p. 139ff.

62. Anderson, Neil. *Victory over the Darkness*, p. 173.

63. Ibid., p. 171.

64. Catherine of Genoa. *Devotional Classics*, edited by Richard Foster and James Bryan Smith. New York, NY: HarperCollins Publishers, 1990, p. 182.

65. Chole, Alicia. *Anonymous: Jesus' hidden years . . . and yours*, Kindle location 923.

66. Leaf, Caroline. *Switch On Your Brain*, p. 66.

67. Ibid., p. 181.

68. Backus, William and Marie Chapian. *Telling Yourself the Truth*, p. 50.

69. Leaf, Caroline. *Switch On Your Brain*, p. 102.

70. https://drleaf.com/media/dr-leaf-i-cant/

71. Chole, Alicia. *Anonymous: Jesus' hidden years . . . and yours*, Kindle location 1141.

72. Ibid., Kindle location 1325.

73. Ibid., Kindle location 1450.

74. Gilder, George. *Wealth and Poverty*. Washington, DC: Regnery Publishing, Inc., 2012. p. 150.

75. Tozer, A. W. *The Divine Conquest*, p. 51.

76. Chole, Alicia. *Anonymous: Jesus' hidden years . . . and yours*, Kindle location 1986.

77. Francisco, Don. *Jesus Is Lord of the Way I Feel*. Nashville, TN, NewPax Records, 1978.

78. Backus, William and Marie Chapian. *Telling Yourself the Truth*, p. 105-106, 109-110, 118.

79. Murphy, Ed. *The Handbook of Spiritual Warfare*, p. 408-409.

80. Anderson, Neil. *Victory over the Darkness*, p. 52-53.

81. Davis, Don L. *Compelling Testimony: Maintaining a Disciplined Walk, Christlike Character, and Godly Relationships as God's Servant*. Wichita, KS: The Urban Ministry Institute, 2006.

82. Moreland, J. P. *The God Question*, p. 203-204.

83. Willard, Dallas. *The Divine Conspiracy*, p. 353-360.

84. Jennings, Timothy R., MD. *The God-Shaped Brain: How Changing Your View of God Transforms Your Life*, p. 58.

85. Kempis, Thomas à. *Devotional Classics*, edited by Richard Foster and James Bryan Smith. New York, NY: HarperCollins Publishers, 1990, p. 154.

86. Lasch, Christopher, *The Culture of Narcissism: American Life in an Age of Diminishing Expectations*, New York, NY: W. W. Norton & Company, Revised Edition (1991), p. 4-231.

87. McIntosh, Gary L., and Samuel D. Rima. *Overcoming the Dark Side of Leadership*. Grand Rapids, MI: Baker Books, 2007, pages 115-17.

Made in the USA
Columbia, SC
26 March 2018